Working Papers
Volume I, Chapters 1-12

for use with

FUNDAMENTAL ACCOUNTING PRINCIPLES

15th Edition

Kermit D. Larson
University of Texas at Austin, Emeritus

John J. Wild
University of Wisconsin at Madison

Barbara Chiappetta
Nassau Community College

Prepared by
John J. Wild
University of Wisconsin at Madison

**Irwin
McGraw-Hill**

**Boston   Burr Ridge, IL   Dubuque, IA   Madison, WI   New York   San Francisco   St. Louis
Bangkok   Bogotá   Caracas   Lisbon   London   Madrid
Mexico City   Milan   New Delhi   Seoul   Singapore   Sydney   Taipei   Toronto**

Irwin/McGraw-Hill

A Division of The McGraw-Hill Companies

Working Papers, Volume I, Chapters 1-12 for use with
FUNDAMENTAL ACCOUNTING PRINCIPLES

7 8 9 0 QPD/QPD 9 4 3 2 1 0

ISBN 0-07-030737-7

http://www.mhhe.com

TABLE OF CONTENTS

Chapter 1:   Accounting in the Information Age 1

Chapter 2:   Financial Statements and Accounting Transactions 13

Chapter 3:   Analyzing and Recording Transactions 41

Chapter 4:   Adjusting Accounts for Financial Statements 91

Chapter 5:   Completing the Accounting Cycle 139

Chapter 6:   Accounting for Merchandising Activities 199

Chapter 7:   Merchandise Inventories and Cost of Sales 259

Chapter 8:   Accounting Information Systems 291

Chapter 9:   Internal Control and Cash 371

Chapter 10: Receivables and Short-Term Investments 395

Chapter 11: Plant Assets, Natural Resources, and Intangible Assets 423

Chapter 12: Current and Long-Term Liabilities 455

Appendix B: Accounting Concepts and Alternative Valuations 491

Appendix C: Present and Future Values 495

_____
_____
_____
_____
_____
_____
_____
_____

Quick Study 1-2

_____
_____
_____
_____
_____
_____
_____

Quick Study 1-3

_____
_____
_____
_____
_____

Quick Study 1-4

_____
_____
_____
_____
_____
_____
_____
_____
_____
_____
_____

_____
_____
_____
_____
_____
_____
_____
_____

Quick Study 1-6

(a)   (1) _____
      (2) _____
      (3) _____

(b)

Assets	=	Liabilities	+	Equity
	=		+	

Exercise 1-1

(a) _____
(b) _____
(c) _____
(d) _____
(e) _____
(f) _____
(g) _____

Exercise 1-2

(a) _____
(b) _____
(c) _____
(d) _____
(e) _____

Exercise 1-3

External User:	_____
	_____
	_____
	_____
	_____

External User:	
External User:	

Exercise 1-4

(1) _____

(2) _____

(3) _____

(4) _____

(5) _____

(6) _____

(7) _____

(8) _____

Exercise 1-5

(a) _____

_____

_____

(b) _____

_____

_____

(c) _____

_____

_____

(d) _____

_____

_____

(1) _____

(2) _____

(3) _____

(4) _____

(5) _____

(6) _____

Exercise 1-7

(1) _____

(2) _____

(3) _____

(4) _____

(5) _____

(6) _____

Exercise 1-8

(a) _____

_____

_____

_____

_____

(b) _____

_____

_____

_____

_____

_____

_____

_____

(c) _____

_____

_____

_____

_____

_____

_____

_____

_____
_____
_____
_____
_____
_____

Exercise 1-10

Assets	=	Liabilities	+	Equity
(a)				
(b)				
(c)				

Problem 1-1 or 1-1A

(1) _____
_____
_____

(2) _____
_____
_____

(3) _____
_____
_____

(4) _____
_____
_____

Problem 1-2 or 1-2A

(1a) _____
_____

(1b) _____
_____
_____

(2) _____
_____
_____

(3) _____
_____
_____

(4) _____
_____
_____
_____
_____
_____

Problem 1-3 or 1-3A

(1) Return: _____
_____

  Risk: _____
_____

(2) Return: _____
_____

  Risk: _____
_____

(3) Return: _____
_____

  Risk: _____
_____

(4) Return: _____
_____

  Risk: _____
_____
_____

(1) Major Activity: _____

_____

_____

(2) Major Activity: _____

_____

_____

(3) Major Activity: _____

_____

_____

_____

Problem 1-4A

I. _____

   A. _____

   B. _____

II. _____

   A. _____

   B. _____

III. _____

   A. _____

   B. _____

_____

Problem 1-5 or 1-5A

(1) _____

(2) _____

(3) _____

(4) _____

(5) _____

(6) _____

(7) _____

(1) _____
_____
_____

(2) _____
_____
_____

(3) _____
_____
_____

(4) _____
_____
_____

(5) Swoosh Ahead: _____
_____
_____
_____

Comparative Analysis

NIKE	REEBOK
(1)	
(2)	
(3)	
(4)	
(5)	

(1) _____
_____
_____
_____
_____

(2) _____
_____
_____
_____
_____

(3) _____
_____
_____
_____
_____

(4) _____
_____
_____
_____
_____

Communicating in Practice

(1) _____
_____
_____
_____
_____
_____

(2) _____
_____
_____
_____
_____
_____

Name _____

(a)

_____

_____

_____

_____

_____

_____

_____

_____

_____

_____

_____

_____

_____

_____

(b)

_____

_____

_____

_____

_____

_____

_____

_____

_____

Teamwork in Action

(1) Meeting Time and Place: _____

_____

(2) Telephone and E-mail Addresses: _____

_____

_____

(3) Instructor Notification: ☐ Yes _____

_____

Name _____

(1) _____

_____
_____
_____
_____
_____
_____
_____
_____
_____
_____
_____

(2) _____

_____
_____
_____
_____
_____
_____
_____
_____
_____
_____
_____

(3) _____

_____
_____
_____
_____
_____
_____
_____
_____
_____
_____
_____

(1)

1	
2	
3	
4	
5	
6	
7	
8	
9	
10	

(2)

1	
2	
3	
4	
5	
6	
7	
8	
9	
10	

(3)

1	
2	
3	
4	
5	
6	
7	
8	
9	
10	

(a) _____

(b) _____

(c) _____

(d) _____

(e) _____

(f) _____

(g) _____

(h) _____

Quick Study 2-2

(a) _____

(b) _____

(c) _____

Quick Study 2-3

Assets	=	Liabilities	+	Equity
(a)				
(b)				
(c)				

Quick Study 2-4

Assets	=	Liabilities	+	Equity
(a)				
(b)				
(c)				

Quick Study 2-5

Return on Equity: _____

_____

_____

_____

_____

_____

(a) _____

_____

(b) _____

_____

(c) _____

_____

(d) _____

_____

(e) _____

_____

_____

Exercise 2-2

(a) _____

_____

(b) _____

_____

(c) _____

_____

(d) _____

_____

(e) _____

_____

_____

(a) Net Income (Loss) = ☐
    Supporting Computations: _____

_____

_____

_____

_____

_____

_____

_____

_____

_____

(b) Net Income (Loss) = ☐
    Supporting Computations: _____

_____

_____

_____

_____

_____

_____

_____

_____

_____

(c) Net Income (Loss) = ☐
    Supporting Computations: _____

_____

_____

_____

_____

_____

_____

_____

_____

(d) Net Income (Loss) = ☐
    Supporting Computations: _____

_____

_____

_____

_____

_____

_____

_____

_____

_____

	CASH	+	ACCOUNTS RECEIVABLE	+	EQUIPMENT	+	ACCOUNTS PAYABLE	+	L. CHAMPION, CAPITAL	EXPLANATION OF CAPITAL
(a)										
(b)										
(c)										
(d)										
(e)										
(f)										
(g)										
(h)										
(i)										
(j)										

Modified Return on Equity:

_____
_____
_____
_____
_____
_____
_____
_____
_____

(a) _____

(b) _____

(c) _____

(d) _____

(e) _____

(f) _____

(g) _____

Exercise 2-6

_____

_____

Exercise 2-8

_____

_____

(1) _____

(2) _____

(3) _____

(4) _____

(5) _____

(6) _____

(7) _____

(8) _____

Exercise 2-10

	(a)	(b)	(c)	(d)

Exercise 2-11

(1) _____

(2) _____

(3) _____

(4) _____

(5) _____

(6) _____

(7) _____

	(a)	(b)	(c)	(d)
Return on Equity:				
Modified Return on Equity:				

Exercise 2-13

(1) _____

(2) _____

(3) _____

(4) _____

(5) _____

(6) _____

(7) _____

(8) _____

	ASSETS						=	LIABILITIES		+	OWNER'S EQUITY	
CASH	+	ACCOUNTS RECEIVABLE	+	OFFICE SUPPLIES	+	OFFICE EQUIPMENT	+	BUILDING	=	ACCOUNTS PAYABLE	+	NOTES PAYABLE	+	CAPITAL	EXPLANATION OF CHANGE
(a)												
(b)												
Bal.												
(c)												
Bal.												
(d)												
Bal.												
(e)												
Bal.												
(f)												
Bal.												
(g)												
Bal.												
(h)												
Bal.												
(i)												
Bal.												
(j)												
Bal.												
(k)												
Bal.												

Part 3

Net Income: _____

_____

_____

_____

_____

_____

Part 4

Return on Equity: _____

_____

_____

_____

Modified Return on Equity: _____

_____

_____

_____

_____

_____

| DATE | ASSETS | | | | | = | LIABILITIES | + | OWNER'S EQUITY | |
	CASH	ACCOUNTS RECEIVABLE	+	PREPAID INSURANCE	+	OFFICE SUPPLIES	=	ACCOUNTS PAYABLE	+	CAPITAL	EXPLANATION OF CHANGE

_____
_____
_____

_____
_____
_____

_____
_____

_____
_____

_____

Part 2

Net Income Computation: _____
_____
_____
_____
_____
_____
_____
_____
_____
_____
_____

Return on Equity: _____

_____

_____

Modified Return on Equity: _____

_____

_____

_____

| DATE | ASSETS | | | | | = | LIABILITIES | + | OWNER'S EQUITY | |
| | CASH | + | ACCOUNTS RECEIVABLE | + | OFFICE SUPPLIES | + | OFFICE EQUIPMENT | + | ELECTRICAL EQUIPMENT | = | ACCOUNTS PAYABLE | + | CAPITAL | | EXPLANATION OF CHANGE |

Part 4

Return on Equity: _____

_____

_____

_____

Part 5

_____

_____

_____

_____

_____

_____

_____

_____

_____

_____

Problem 2-5 or 2-5A
Part 1: Company _____

(a) _____

_____

_____

_____

_____

(b) _____

_____

_____

_____

_____

_____

_____

(c) _____

_____

_____

_____

_____

_____

Part 2: Company _____

(a)
_____
_____
_____
_____

(b)
_____
_____
_____

(c)
_____
_____
_____
_____
_____

Part 3: Company _____

_____
_____
_____
_____
_____
_____
_____
_____
_____
_____
_____
_____
_____
_____
_____
_____
_____
_____
_____
_____
_____
_____

Part 4: Company _____

_____

_____

_____

_____

_____

_____

_____

_____

_____

_____

_____

_____

_____

_____

_____

_____

_____

_____

_____

_____

_____

Part 5: Company _____

_____

_____

_____

_____

_____

_____

_____

_____

_____

_____

_____

_____

_____

_____

_____

_____

_____

_____

_____

_____

TRANSACTION	BALANCE SHEET			INCOME STMT.	STATEMENT OF CASH FLOWS		
	TOTAL ASSETS	TOTAL LIABILITIES	EQUITY	NET INCOME	OPERATING	FINANCING	INVESTING
1.							
2.							
3.							
4.							
5.							
6.							
7.							
8.							
9.							
10.							

Reporting in Action

(1) _____

_____

(2) _____

_____

(3) _____

_____

(4) _____

_____

_____

(5) _____
_____
_____

(6) _____
_____
_____

(7) _____
_____
_____

(8) _____
_____
_____

(9) _____
_____
_____

(10) _____
_____
_____

(11) Swoosh Ahead: _____
_____
_____
_____
_____
_____

(1a) _____

_____

(1b) _____

_____

(2) _____

_____

_____

(3) _____

_____

_____

(4) _____

_____

_____

_____

Ethics Challenge

(1) _____

_____

_____

_____

_____

(2) _____

_____

_____

_____

_____

(3) _____

_____

_____

_____

_____

(4) _____

_____

_____

_____

_____

_____

(1) _____

_____

_____

_____

_____

_____

_____

_____

_____

_____

_____

_____

_____

_____

(2) _____

_____

_____

_____

_____

_____

_____

_____

_____

_____

_____

_____

_____

(3) _____

_____

_____

_____

_____

_____

_____

_____

_____

_____

_____

_____

_____

_____

_____

_____

(1) _____

_____

(2) _____

_____

_____

_____

_____

_____

_____

_____

_____

Teamwork in Action
Part 1

(a) _____

_____

_____

(b) _____

_____

_____

(c) _____

_____

_____

(d) _____

_____

_____

_____
_____
_____
_____
_____
_____
_____
_____
_____
_____
_____
_____
_____
_____

Part 3

_____
_____
_____
_____
_____
_____
_____
_____
_____
_____
_____
_____
_____

Hitting the Road

Company Annual Report Information:

_____
_____
_____
_____
_____
_____
_____
_____

(1) _____

_____

_____

(2) _____

_____

_____

(3) _____

_____

_____

(4) _____

_____

_____

Source Documents are: _____

_____

_____

_____

_____

Quick Study 3-2

(a) _____

(b) _____

(c) _____

(d) _____

(e) _____

(f) _____

(g) _____

(h) _____

(i) _____

(j) _____

Quick Study 3-3

(a) _____

(b) _____

(c) _____

(d) _____

(e) _____

(f) _____

(g) _____

(h) _____

(i) _____

(j) _____

Quick Study 3-4

(a) _____

(b) _____

(c) _____

(d) _____

(e) _____

(f) _____

(g) _____

(h) _____

(i) _____

(j) _____

GENERAL JOURNAL

Date	Account Titles and Explanation	Post Ref.	Debit	Credit

Quick Study 3-6

_____
_____
_____
_____
_____

Exercise 3-1

ACCOUNT	TYPE OF ACCOUNT	DEBIT OR CREDIT INCREASE	DEBIT OR CREDIT DECREASE	NORMAL BALANCE
a.				
b.				
c.				
d.				
e.				
f.				
g.				
h.				
i.				
j.				
k.				
l.				

_____
_____
_____
_____
_____
_____
_____
_____
_____
_____
_____
_____
_____
_____
_____
_____
_____
_____
_____
_____

Exercise 3-3

Cash	Accounts Payable

	Steve Moore, Capital

Accounts Receivable	Steve Moore, Withdrawals

Office Supplies	Fees Earned

Office Equipment	Rent Expense

	Description	(1) Difference between Debit and Credit Column	(2) Column with the Larger Total	(3) Identify account(s) incorrectly stated	(4) Amount that account(s) is overstated or understated
(a)		$810	Credit	Rent Expense	Rent Expense is understated by $810
(b)					
(c)					
(d)					
(e)					
(f)					
(g)					

(a) _____

_____

_____

(b) _____

_____

_____

(c) _____

_____

_____

(d) _____

_____

_____

(e) _____

_____

_____

_____

_____

_____

List of Errors:

_____

_____

_____

_____

_____

_____

_____

_____

_____

_____

_____

_____

(1) _____

_____

_____

_____

_____

_____

_____

(2) _____

_____

_____

_____

_____

_____

_____

(3) _____

_____

_____

_____

_____

_____

_____

Exercise 3-9

(a) _____

(b) _____

(c) _____

(d) _____

(e) _____

(f) _____

(g) _____

GENERAL JOURNAL

Date	Account Titles and Explanation	Post Ref.	Debit	Credit
(a)				
(b)				
(c)				
(d)				
(e)				
(f)				
(g)				

GENERAL JOURNAL

Date	Account Titles and Explanation	Post Ref.	Debit	Credit

Cash	**Photography Equipment**
	Hannah Young, Capital
	Photography Fees Earned
Office Supplies	**Utilities Expense**
Prepaid Rent	

GENERAL JOURNAL

Date		Account Titles and Explanation	Post Ref.	Debit			Credit		

Transactions not creating revenue and the reasons:

_____
_____
_____
_____
_____
_____
_____
_____
_____
_____
_____
_____
_____
_____
_____
_____
_____
_____

GENERAL JOURNAL

Date	Account Titles and Explanation	Post Ref.	Debit	Credit

Transactions not creating expense and the reasons:

_____
_____
_____
_____
_____
_____
_____
_____
_____
_____
_____
_____
_____

Part 1

(1) _____

(2) _____

(3) _____

(4) _____

(5) _____

(6) _____

Part 2

_____

_____

_____

_____

_____

Part 3

_____

_____

_____

_____

_____

Part 4

_____

_____

_____

_____

_____

Name _____

Cash	Land

	Accounts Payable

	Long-Term Notes Payable

Accounts Receivable	_____, Capital

Office Supplies	_____, Withdrawals

Automobiles	Fees Earned

Office Equipment	Salaries Expense

	Utilities Expense

Building	

_____   _____
Cash   **Accounts Payable**

_____   _____
Accounts Receivable   **Long-Term Notes Payable**

_____   _____ , **Capital**

_____   _____ , **Withdrawals**
Prepaid Insurance

                                           _____ **Fees Earned**

_____   _____
Office Equipment   **Wages Expense**

_____   _____ **Rental Expense**
Equipment

                                           _____
                                           Advertising Expense

Building
_____
|

Land   Repairs Expense
_____   _____
| |

_____

_____

_____

Part 3

_____

_____

_____

_____

_____

_____

_____

_____

GENERAL JOURNAL

Date	Account Titles and Explanation	Post Ref.	Debit	Credit

Date	Account Titles and Explanation	Post Ref.	Debit	Credit

GENERAL LEDGER

Cash   ACCOUNT NO. 101

DATE	EXPLANATION	P.R.	DEBIT	CREDIT	BALANCE

Accounts Receivable   ACCOUNT NO. 106

DATE	EXPLANATION	P.R.	DEBIT	CREDIT	BALANCE

Office Supplies   ACCOUNT NO. 124

DATE	EXPLANATION	P.R.	DEBIT	CREDIT	BALANCE

Prepaid Insurance   ACCOUNT NO. 128

DATE	EXPLANATION	P.R.	DEBIT	CREDIT	BALANCE

Name _____

Prepaid Rent   ACCOUNT NO. 131

DATE	EXPLANATION	P.R.	DEBIT	CREDIT	BALANCE

Office Equipment   ACCOUNT NO. 163

DATE	EXPLANATION	P.R.	DEBIT	CREDIT	BALANCE

Accounts Payable   ACCOUNT NO. 201

DATE	EXPLANATION	P.R.	DEBIT	CREDIT	BALANCE

_____, **Capital**   ACCOUNT NO. 301

DATE	EXPLANATION	P.R.	DEBIT	CREDIT	BALANCE

_____, **Withdrawals**   ACCOUNT NO. 302

DATE	EXPLANATION	P.R.	DEBIT	CREDIT	BALANCE

Service Fees Earned**   ACCOUNT NO. 401

DATE	EXPLANATION	P.R.	DEBIT	CREDIT	BALANCE

Services Revenue*   ACCOUNT NO. 403

DATE	EXPLANATION	P.R.	DEBIT	CREDIT	BALANCE

Utilities Expense   ACCOUNT NO. 690

DATE	EXPLANATION	P.R.	DEBIT	CREDIT	BALANCE

* Problem 3-3 only.
** Problem 3-3A only.

GENERAL LEDGER

Cash   ACCOUNT NO. 101

DATE	EXPLANATION	P.R.	DEBIT	CREDIT	BALANCE

Accounts Receivable   ACCOUNT NO. 106

DATE	EXPLANATION	P.R.	DEBIT	CREDIT	BALANCE

Office Supplies   ACCOUNT NO. 124

DATE	EXPLANATION	P.R.	DEBIT	CREDIT	BALANCE

Prepaid Insurance   ACCOUNT NO. 128

DATE	EXPLANATION	P.R.	DEBIT	CREDIT	BALANCE

Automobiles**   ACCOUNT NO. 151

DATE	EXPLANATION	P.R.	DEBIT	CREDIT	BALANCE

Trucks*   ACCOUNT NO. 153

DATE	EXPLANATION	P.R.	DEBIT	CREDIT	BALANCE

Office Equipment   ACCOUNT NO. 163

DATE	EXPLANATION	P.R.	DEBIT	CREDIT	BALANCE

Store Equipment**   ACCOUNT NO. 165

DATE	EXPLANATION	P.R.	DEBIT	CREDIT	BALANCE

Moving Equipment*   ACCOUNT NO. 167

DATE	EXPLANATION	P.R.	DEBIT	CREDIT	BALANCE

* Problem 3-4 only.
** Problem 3-4A only.

Accounts Payable   ACCOUNT NO. 201

DATE	EXPLANATION	P.R.	DEBIT	CREDIT	BALANCE

_____, **Capital**   ACCOUNT NO. 301

DATE	EXPLANATION	P.R.	DEBIT	CREDIT	BALANCE

_____, **Withdrawals**   ACCOUNT NO. 302

DATE	EXPLANATION	P.R.	DEBIT	CREDIT	BALANCE

_____ **Fees Earned**   ACCOUNT NO. 401

DATE	EXPLANATION	P.R.	DEBIT	CREDIT	BALANCE

Salaries Expense [**]   ACCOUNT No. 622

DATE	EXPLANATION	P.R.	DEBIT	CREDIT	BALANCE

Wages Expense [*]   ACCOUNT No. 623

DATE	EXPLANATION	P.R.	DEBIT	CREDIT	BALANCE

Part 2
Explanation for the Journal Entries:

_____
_____
_____
_____
_____
_____
_____
_____
_____
_____
_____
_____
_____
_____
_____
_____
_____
_____
_____
_____
_____
_____
_____
_____
_____
_____
_____
_____

_____

[*] Problem 3-4 only.
[**] Problem 3-4A only.

Errors in Original Trial Balance:

_____
_____
_____

Part 2
Seven Most Likely Transactions: _____
_____
_____
_____
_____
_____
_____
_____
_____
_____
_____
_____
_____
_____
_____
_____
_____
_____
_____
_____

Schedule of Cash Received and Paid. _____

_____
_____
_____
_____
_____
_____
_____
_____
_____
_____
_____
_____
_____
_____
_____
_____
_____
_____
_____

Balance Sheet

Name _____

GENERAL JOURNAL

Date	Account Titles and Explanation	Post Ref.	Debit	Credit

Date	Account Titles and Explanation	Post Ref.	Debit	Credit

Date	Account Titles and Explanation	Post Ref.	Debit	Credit

GENERAL LEDGER

Cash   ACCOUNT NO. 101

DATE	EXPLANATION	P.R.	DEBIT	CREDIT	BALANCE

Accounts Receivable   ACCOUNT NO. 106

DATE	EXPLANATION	P.R.	DEBIT	CREDIT	BALANCE

Computer Supplies   ACCOUNT NO. 126

DATE	EXPLANATION	P.R.	DEBIT	CREDIT	BALANCE

Prepaid Insurance   ACCOUNT NO. 128

DATE	EXPLANATION	P.R.	DEBIT	CREDIT	BALANCE

Prepaid Rent   ACCOUNT NO. 131

DATE	EXPLANATION	P.R.	DEBIT	CREDIT	BALANCE

Office Equipment   ACCOUNT NO. 163

DATE	EXPLANATION	P.R.	DEBIT	CREDIT	BALANCE

Computer Equipment   ACCOUNT NO. 167

DATE	EXPLANATION	P.R.	DEBIT	CREDIT	BALANCE

Accounts Payable   ACCOUNT NO. 201

DATE	EXPLANATION	P.R.	DEBIT	CREDIT	BALANCE

Mary Graham, Capital   ACCOUNT NO. 301

DATE	EXPLANATION	P.R.	DEBIT	CREDIT	BALANCE

Mary Graham, Withdrawals   ACCOUNT NO. 302

DATE	EXPLANATION	P.R.	DEBIT	CREDIT	BALANCE

Computer Services Revenue   ACCOUNT NO. 403

DATE	EXPLANATION	P.R.	DEBIT	CREDIT	BALANCE

Wages Expense   ACCOUNT NO. 623

DATE	EXPLANATION	P.R.	DEBIT	CREDIT	BALANCE

Advertising Expense   ACCOUNT NO. 655

DATE	EXPLANATION	P.R.	DEBIT	CREDIT	BALANCE

Mileage Expense   ACCOUNT NO. 676

DATE	EXPLANATION	P.R.	DEBIT	CREDIT	BALANCE

Name _____

Miscellaneous Expense   ACCOUNT NO. 677

DATE	EXPLANATION	P.R.	DEBIT	CREDIT	BALANCE

Repairs Expense, Computer   ACCOUNT NO. 684

DATE	EXPLANATION	P.R.	DEBIT	CREDIT	BALANCE

(1) _____
_____

(2) _____
_____
_____
_____
_____
_____

(3) _____
_____
_____
_____
_____
_____

(4) _____
_____
_____

(5) _____
_____
_____

(6) _____
_____
_____
_____
_____
_____

(7) Swoosh Ahead: _____
_____
_____
_____
_____
_____

(1) _____

_____

_____

_____

(2) _____

_____

_____

_____

(3) _____

_____

_____

_____

Ethics Challenge

_____

_____

_____

_____

_____

_____

_____

_____

_____

_____

_____

_____

_____

_____

_____

_____

_____

_____

(1) _____

_____

_____

_____

_____

_____

(2) _____

_____

_____

_____

_____

_____

_____

_____

_____

_____

_____

_____

_____

_____

_____

_____

_____

_____

_____

_____

_____

_____

_____

_____

_____

_____

_____

_____

_____

_____

_____

_____

(1) _____

_____

_____

_____

_____

_____

(2) _____

_____

_____

_____

_____

_____

(1) _____

(a) _____

_____

(b) _____

_____

(c) _____

_____

(d) _____

_____

(e) _____

_____

(f) _____

_____

(g) _____

_____

(h) _____

_____

(i) _____

_____

(j) _____

_____

(2) _____

_____

_____

_____

(3) _____

_____

_____

_____

(4) _____

_____

_____

_____

_____

_____

(5) _____

_____

_____

_____

_____

_____

_____

_____

_____

_____

_____

_____

_____

(6) _____

_____

_____

_____

_____

_____

(7) _____

_____

_____

_____

_____

_____

_____

_____

_____

_____

_____

_____

_____

_____

_____

(1) _____

(2) _____

(3) _____

(4) _____

(1) _____

_____

_____

_____

_____

_____

_____

_____

_____

_____

_____

_____

(2) _____

_____

_____

_____

_____

_____

(3) _____

_____

_____

_____

_____

_____

_____

(4) _____

_____

_____

_____

_____

_____

_____

Cash Basis: _____

_____

_____

_____

_____

Accrual Basis: _____

_____

_____

_____

_____

Quick Study 4-2

Debit	Credit

(a) _____

(b) _____

(c) _____

Quick Study 4-3

Answer is _____

_____

_____

_____

_____

_____

_____

Quick Study 4-4

Answer is _____

_____

_____

_____

_____

_____

Quick Study 4-5

Answer is _____

_____

_____

_____

_____

Profit Margin: _____

_____

_____

_____

_____

Interpretation of Profit Margin: _____

_____

_____

_____

_____

_____

Quick Study 4-7

(a) _____

(b) _____

(c) _____

(d) _____

(e) _____

Quick Study 4-8

	Dr./Cr.	Account Titles	Statement
(a)	Debit		
	Credit		
(b)	Debit		
	Credit		
(c)	Debit		
	Credit		
(d)	Debit		
	Credit		
(e)	Debit		
	Credit		

GENERAL JOURNAL

Date	Account Titles and Explanation	Post Ref.	Debit	Credit
(a)				
(b)				
(c)				
(d)				
(e)				
(f)				

Adjusting Entry:

GENERAL JOURNAL

Date	Account Titles and Explanation	Post Ref.	Debit	Credit

Payday Entry:

GENERAL JOURNAL

Date	Account Titles and Explanation	Post Ref.	Debit	Credit

Exercise 4-3

(1) _____

(2) _____

(3) _____

(4) _____

(5) _____

(6) _____

(a)

_____

_____

_____

(b)

_____

_____

_____

(c)

_____

_____

_____

(d)

_____

_____

_____

Exercise 4-5

(a)
Adjusting Entry:

GENERAL JOURNAL

Date	Account Titles and Explanation	Post Ref.	Debit	Credit

Journal Entry (Next Period):

GENERAL JOURNAL

Date	Account Titles and Explanation	Post Ref.	Debit	Credit

(b)
Adjusting Entry:

GENERAL JOURNAL

Date	Account Titles and Explanation	Post Ref.	Debit	Credit

Journal Entry (Next Period):

GENERAL JOURNAL

Date	Account Titles and Explanation	Post Ref.	Debit	Credit

(c)
Adjusting Entry:

GENERAL JOURNAL

Date	Account Titles and Explanation	Post Ref.	Debit	Credit

Journal Entry (Next Period):

GENERAL JOURNAL

Date	Account Titles and Explanation	Post Ref.	Debit	Credit

Balance Sheet Asset under the:				Insurance Expense under the:		
Date of:	Accrual Basis	Cash Basis		Year	Accrual Basis	Cash Basis
12/31/1999				1999		
12/31/2000				2000		
12/31/2001				2001		
12/31/2002				2002		
				Total		

Workspace:

(a)

GENERAL JOURNAL

Date		Account Titles and Explanation	Post Ref.	Debit			Credit		

(b)

GENERAL JOURNAL

Date		Account Titles and Explanation	Post Ref.	Debit			Credit		

(c)

GENERAL JOURNAL

Date		Account Titles and Explanation	Post Ref.	Debit			Credit		

GENERAL JOURNAL

Date	Account Titles and Explanation	Post Ref.	Debit	Credit

Date	Account Titles and Explanation	Post Ref.	Debit			Credit		
(a)								
(b)								
(c)								
(d)								
(e)								
(f)								
(g)								

(a)

GENERAL JOURNAL

Date	Account Titles and Explanation	Post Ref.	Debit	Credit

(b)

GENERAL JOURNAL

Date	Account Titles and Explanation	Post Ref.	Debit	Credit

(c)
Method in Part (a):
    Unearned Fees = $_____.

        Fees Earned = $ _____.

Method in Part (b):
    Unearned Fees = $_____.

        Fees Earned = $ _____.

Exercise 4-11
Profit Margin Calculation:

(a) _____
_____
(b) _____
_____
(c) _____
_____
(d) _____
_____
(e) _____
_____

Most Profitable: _____
_____

Interpretation of Profit Margin: _____
_____
_____

GENERAL JOURNAL

Date	Account Titles and Explanation	Post Ref.	Debit	Credit

GENERAL JOURNAL

Date	Account Titles and Explanation	Post Ref.	Debit	Credit

Cash
_____

Accts. Receivable
_____

Teaching Supplies
_____

Prepaid Insurance
_____

Prepaid Rent
_____

Professional Library
_____

Accumulated Depreciation,
Professional Library
_____

Equipment
_____

Accumulated Depreciation,
Equipment
_____

Accounts Payable
_____

Salaries Payable
_____

Unearned Training Fees
_____

_____ , Capital
_____

_____ , Withdrawals
_____

Tuition Fees Earned

Teaching Supplies Expense

Training Fees Earned

Advertising Expense

Utilities Expense

Depreciation Expense,
Equipment

Depreciation Expense
Professional Library

Salaries Expense

Insurance Expense

Rent Expense

GENERAL JOURNAL

Date	Account Titles and Explanation	Post Ref.	Debit	Credit

Adjusted Trial Balance

Income Statement

Statement of Changes in Owner's Equity

Balance Sheet

Part 5

Profit Margin:

Income Statement

Statement of Changes in Owner's Equity

Balance Sheet

Part 3

Profit Margin*:

* This is the modified profit margin for Problem 4-3A.

ACCOUNT TITLES	UNADJUSTED TRIAL BALANCE		ADJUSTMENTS		ADJUSTED TRIAL BALANCE	
	DR	CR	DR	CR	DR	CR

(a) _____

(b) _____

(c) _____

(d) _____

(e) _____

(f) _____

(g) _____

(h) _____

Accrual Basis Income Statement

Conversion of Cash Inflows to Accrual Basis Revenues:

Conversion of Cash Outflows to Accrual Basis Expenses:

(1) _____	(7) _____
(2) _____	(8) _____
(3) _____	(9) _____
(4) _____	(10) _____
(5) _____	(11) _____
(6) _____	(12) _____

Problem 4-6 or 4-6A
Part 1

Income Statement

Statement of Changes in Owner's Equity

Balance Sheet

Part 2

Modified Profit Margin:

GENERAL JOURNAL

Date	Account Titles and Explanation	Post Ref.	Debit	Credit

GENERAL JOURNAL

Date	Account Titles and Explanation	Post Ref.	Debit	Credit

GENERAL JOURNAL

Date	Account Titles and Explanation	Post Ref.	Debit	Credit

Chapter 4
Part 2

Serial Problem
Echo Systems
Adjusting Entries

Name _____

GENERAL JOURNAL

Date	Account Titles and Explanation	Post Ref.	Debit	Credit

Chapter 4
Part 2
   Serial Problem
   Echo Systems
   (Continued)

Name _____

GENERAL LEDGER

Cash   ACCOUNT NO. 101

DATE	EXPLANATION	P.R.	DEBIT	CREDIT	BALANCE
2000 Nov. 30	Balance				35 720 00

Accounts Receivable   ACCOUNT NO. 106

DATE	EXPLANATION	P.R.	DEBIT	CREDIT	BALANCE
2000 Nov. 30	Balance				9 450 00

Computer Supplies   ACCOUNT NO. 126

DATE	EXPLANATION	P.R.	DEBIT	CREDIT	BALANCE
2000 Nov. 30	Balance				2 280 00

Chapter 4
Part 2

Serial Problem
Echo Systems
(Continued)

Name _____

Prepaid Insurance — ACCOUNT NO. 128

DATE	EXPLANATION	P.R.	DEBIT	CREDIT	BALANCE
2000 Nov. 30	Balance				2 160 00

Prepaid Rent — ACCOUNT NO. 131

DATE	EXPLANATION	P.R.	DEBIT	CREDIT	BALANCE
2000 Nov. 30	Balance				4 500 00

Office Equipment — ACCOUNT NO. 163

DATE	EXPLANATION	P.R.	DEBIT	CREDIT	BALANCE
2000 Nov. 30	Balance				9 000 00

Accumulated Depreciation, Office Equipment — ACCOUNT NO. 164

DATE	EXPLANATION	P.R.	DEBIT	CREDIT	BALANCE

Computer Equipment　　　　ACCOUNT NO. 167

DATE	EXPLANATION	P.R.	DEBIT	CREDIT	BALANCE
2000 Nov. 30	Balance				18 000 00

Accumulated Depreciation, Computer Equipment　　　ACCOUNT NO. 168

DATE	EXPLANATION	P.R.	DEBIT	CREDIT	BALANCE

Accounts Payable　　　　ACCOUNT NO. 201

DATE	EXPLANATION	P.R.	DEBIT	CREDIT	BALANCE
2000 Nov. 30	Balance				-0-

Wages Payable　　　　ACCOUNT NO. 210

DATE	EXPLANATION	P.R.	DEBIT	CREDIT	BALANCE

Unearned Computer Services Revenue　　　ACCOUNT NO. 236

DATE	EXPLANATION	P.R.	DEBIT	CREDIT	BALANCE

Chapter 4   **Serial Problem**   *Name*
Part 2   **Echo Systems**
         (Continued)

Mary Graham, Capital   ACCOUNT NO. 301

DATE	EXPLANATION	P.R.	DEBIT	CREDIT	BALANCE
2000 Nov. 30	Balance				72 000 00

Mary Graham, Withdrawals   ACCOUNT NO. 302

DATE	EXPLANATION	P.R.	DEBIT	CREDIT	BALANCE
2000 Nov. 30	Balance				5 400 00

Computer Services Revenue   ACCOUNT NO. 403

DATE	EXPLANATION	P.R.	DEBIT	CREDIT	BALANCE
2000 Nov. 30	Balance				20 475 00

Depreciation Expense, Office Equipment   ACCOUNT NO. 612

DATE	EXPLANATION	P.R.	DEBIT	CREDIT	BALANCE

Depreciation Expense, Computer Equipment   ACCOUNT NO. 613

DATE	EXPLANATION	P.R.	DEBIT	CREDIT	BALANCE

Chapter 4
Part 2

Serial Problem
Echo Systems
(Continued)

Name _____

Wages Expense   ACCOUNT NO. 623

DATE	EXPLANATION	P.R.	DEBIT	CREDIT	BALANCE
2000 Nov. 30	Balance				2 100 00

Insurance Expense   ACCOUNT NO. 637

DATE	EXPLANATION	P.R.	DEBIT	CREDIT	BALANCE

Rent Expense   ACCOUNT NO. 640

DATE	EXPLANATION	P.R.	DEBIT	CREDIT	BALANCE

Computer Supplies Expense   ACCOUNT NO. 652

DATE	EXPLANATION	P.R.	DEBIT	CREDIT	BALANCE

Advertising Expense   ACCOUNT NO. 655

DATE	EXPLANATION	P.R.	DEBIT	CREDIT	BALANCE
2000 Nov. 30	Balance				1 860 00

Mileage Expense   ACCOUNT NO. 676

DATE	EXPLANATION	P.R.	DEBIT	CREDIT	BALANCE
2000 Nov. 30	Balance				550 00

Miscellaneous Expense   ACCOUNT NO. 677

DATE	EXPLANATION	P.R.	DEBIT	CREDIT	BALANCE
2000 Nov. 30	Balance				750 00

Repairs Expense, Computer   ACCOUNT NO. 684

DATE	EXPLANATION	P.R.	DEBIT	CREDIT	BALANCE
2000 Nov. 30	Balance				705 00

ECHO SYSTEMS
Adjusted Trial Balance
December 31, 2000

ECHO SYSTEMS
Income Statement
For Three Months Ended December 31, 2000

Part 5

ECHO SYSTEMS
Statement of Changes in Owner's Equity
For Three Months Ended December 31, 2000

Chapter 4
Part 6

Serial Problem
Echo Systems
(Continued)

Name _____

ECHO SYSTEMS
Balance Sheet
December 31, 2000

(1) _____
_____
_____

(2) _____
_____
_____
_____
_____

(3) _____
_____
_____
_____
_____
_____

(4) _____
_____
_____
_____
_____
_____
_____
_____

Comparative Analysis

(1) _____
_____
_____
_____
_____
_____
_____
_____

(2) _____
_____
_____
_____
_____
_____

(3) _____
_____
_____
_____
_____

(4) _____
_____
_____
_____

Ethics Challenge

(1) _____
_____
_____
_____
_____
_____
_____
_____

(2) _____
_____
_____
_____
_____
_____
_____
_____
_____
_____

(3) _____

_____

_____

_____

_____

_____

_____

_____

_____

Communicating in Practice

_____

_____

_____

_____

_____

_____

_____

_____

_____

_____

_____

_____

_____

_____

_____

_____

_____

_____

_____

_____

_____

_____

_____

_____

_____

(1) _____
_____
_____
_____
_____

(2)
(a) _____
_____
_____
_____

(b) _____
_____
_____

(c) _____
_____
_____

(d) _____
_____
_____

(e) _____
_____
_____
_____

_____
_____
_____
_____
_____
_____
_____
_____
_____
_____
_____
_____
_____
_____
_____
_____
_____
_____
_____
_____
_____
_____
_____
_____
_____
_____
_____
_____
_____
_____
_____
_____
_____
_____
_____
_____
_____
_____
_____

(1) _____

_____

_____

_____

_____

(2) _____

_____

_____

_____

(3) _____

_____

_____

_____

(4) _____

_____

_____

_____

(5) _____

_____

_____

_____

_____

_____
_____
_____
_____
_____
_____
_____
_____
_____
_____

Quick Study 5-2

Steps

1st _____
2nd _____
3rd _____
4th _____
5th _____
6th _____
7th _____
8th _____
9th _____

Quick Study 5-3

(1) _____
(2) _____
(3) _____
(4) _____
(5) _____
(6) _____
(7) _____

Quick Study 5-4

_____
_____
_____
_____
_____
_____
_____
_____
_____
_____
_____

(1) _____
(2) _____
(3) _____
(4) _____
(5) _____
(6) _____

Quick Study 5-6

_____
_____
_____
_____
_____
_____
_____
_____
_____
_____

Quick Study 5-7

GENERAL JOURNAL

Date	Account Titles and Explanation	Post Ref.	Debit	Credit

GENERAL JOURNAL

Date	Account Titles and Explanation	Post Ref.	Debit	Credit

ACCOUNT TITLES	ADJUSTED TRIAL BALANCE		CLOSING ENTRIES		POST-CLOSING TRIAL BALANCE	
	DR	CR	DR	CR	DR	CR

(a)

GENERAL JOURNAL

Date	Account Titles and Explanation	Post Ref.	Debit	Credit

(b)

_____
_____
_____
_____
_____
_____
_____
_____
_____
_____
_____

GENERAL JOURNAL

Date	Account Titles and Explanation	Post Ref.	Debit	Credit

Posting to Accounts:

M. Jones, Capital

Rent Expense

M. Jones, Withdrawals

Salaries Expense

Income Summary

Insurance Expense

Services Revenue

Depreciation Expense

Balance Sheet

Deshaw Delivery Company

Work Sheet

For the Year Ended December 31, 2000

Account Title	Unadjusted Trial Balance		Adjustments		Adjusted Trial Balance		Income Statement		Statement of Changes in Owner's Equity and Balance Sheet	
	Dr.	Cr.	Dr.	Cr.	Dr.	Cr.	Dr.	Cr.	Dr.	Cr.

_____
_____
_____
_____
_____
_____
_____
_____
_____
_____

Exercise 5-8

	Current Assets	Current Liabilities	Current Ratio
Case 1			
Case 2			
Case 3			
Case 4			
Case 5			

Exercise 5-9

(1)	(5)	(9)	(13)
(2)	(6)	(10)	(14)
(3)	(7)	(11)	(15)
(4)	(8)	(12)	(16)

GENERAL JOURNAL

Date	Account Titles and Explanation	Post Ref.	Debit	Credit

	Debit	Credit

GENERAL JOURNAL

Date	Account Titles and Explanation	Post Ref.	Debit	Credit

ACCOUNT TITLES	ADJUSTED TRIAL BALANCE		INCOME STATEMENT		STATEMENT OF CHANGES IN OWNER'S EQUITY & BALANCE SHEET	
	DR	CR	DR	CR	DR	CR

Exercise 5-13

GENERAL JOURNAL

Date	Account Titles and Explanation	Post Ref.	Debit	Credit

GENERAL JOURNAL

Date	Account Titles and Explanation	Post Ref.	Debit	Credit

Part 2

GENERAL JOURNAL

Date	Account Titles and Explanation	Post Ref.	Debit	Credit

GENERAL JOURNAL

Date	Account Titles and Explanation	Post Ref.	Debit	Credit

Problem 5-1 or 5-1A
Part 1

Income Statement

	Debit	Credit

Statement of Changes in Owner's Equity

Balance Sheet

ACCOUNT TITLES	DR	CR	DR	CR	DR	CR

GENERAL JOURNAL

Date	Account Titles and Explanation	Post Ref.	Debit	Credit

Part 4

Current Ratio:

Problem 5-2 or 5-2A
Part 1

Income Statement

Statement of Changes in Owner's Equity

Balance Sheet

Chapter 5   **Problem 5-2 or 5-2A**   *Name*
Part 2   **(Continued)**
Closing Entries

GENERAL JOURNAL

Date	Account Titles and Explanation	Post Ref.	Debit	Credit

(a) _____

_____

_____

_____

(b) _____

_____

_____

(c) _____

_____

_____

(d) _____

_____

_____

(e) _____

_____

_____

_____

Problem 5-3 or 5-3A
Part 1

GENERAL LEDGER

Cash   **ACCOUNT NO. 101**

DATE	EXPLANATION	P.R.	DEBIT	CREDIT	BALANCE

Accounts Receivable   ACCOUNT NO. 106

DATE	ACCOUNT TITLES AND EXPLANATION	P.R.	DEBIT	CREDIT	BALANCE

Office Supplies   ACCOUNT NO. 124

DATE	ACCOUNT TITLES AND EXPLANATION	P.R.	DEBIT	CREDIT	BALANCE

Prepaid Insurance   ACCOUNT NO. 128

DATE	ACCOUNT TITLES AND EXPLANATION	P.R.	DEBIT	CREDIT	BALANCE

Computer Equipment[*]   ACCOUNT NO. 167

DATE	ACCOUNT TITLES AND EXPLANATION	P.R.	DEBIT	CREDIT	BALANCE

Accumulated Depreciation, Computer Equipment[*]   ACCOUNT NO. 168

DATE	ACCOUNT TITLES AND EXPLANATION	P.R.	DEBIT	CREDIT	BALANCE

Buildings[**]   ACCOUNT NO. 173

DATE	ACCOUNT TITLES AND EXPLANATION	P.R.	DEBIT	CREDIT	BALANCE

Accumulated Depreciation, Buildings[**]   ACCOUNT NO. 174

DATE	ACCOUNT TITLES AND EXPLANATION	P.R.	DEBIT	CREDIT	BALANCE

[*] Problem 5-3 only.
[**] Problem 5-3A only.

Salaries Payable   ACCOUNT NO. 209

DATE	ACCOUNT TITLES AND EXPLANATION	P.R.	DEBIT	CREDIT	BALANCE

_____ **, Capital**   ACCOUNT NO. 301

DATE	ACCOUNT TITLES AND EXPLANATION	P.R.	DEBIT	CREDIT	BALANCE

_____ **, Withdrawals**   ACCOUNT NO. 302

DATE	ACCOUNT TITLES AND EXPLANATION	P.R.	DEBIT	CREDIT	BALANCE

Storage Fees Earned[**]   ACCOUNT NO. 401

DATE	ACCOUNT TITLES AND EXPLANATION	P.R.	DEBIT	CREDIT	BALANCE

Commissions Earned[*]   ACCOUNT NO. 405

DATE	ACCOUNT TITLES AND EXPLANATION	P.R.	DEBIT	CREDIT	BALANCE

[*] Problem 5-3 only.
[**] Problem 5-3A only.

Depreciation Expense, Buildings**   ACCOUNT NO. 606

DATE	ACCOUNT TITLES AND EXPLANATION	P.R.	DEBIT	CREDIT	BALANCE

Depreciation Expense, Computer Equipment*   ACCOUNT NO. 612

DATE	ACCOUNT TITLES AND EXPLANATION	P.R.	DEBIT	CREDIT	BALANCE

Salaries Expense   ACCOUNT NO. 622

DATE	ACCOUNT TITLES AND EXPLANATION	P.R.	DEBIT	CREDIT	BALANCE

Insurance Expense   ACCOUNT NO. 637

DATE	ACCOUNT TITLES AND EXPLANATION	P.R.	DEBIT	CREDIT	BALANCE

Rent Expense   ACCOUNT NO. 640

DATE	ACCOUNT TITLES AND EXPLANATION	P.R.	DEBIT	CREDIT	BALANCE

* Problem 5-3 only.
** Problem 5-3A only.

Office Supplies Expense　　　ACCOUNT NO. 650

DATE	ACCOUNT TITLES AND EXPLANATION	P.R.	DEBIT	CREDIT	BALANCE

Repairs Expense　　　ACCOUNT NO. 684

DATE	ACCOUNT TITLES AND EXPLANATION	P.R.	DEBIT	CREDIT	BALANCE

Telephone Expense　　　ACCOUNT NO. 688

DATE	ACCOUNT TITLES AND EXPLANATION	P.R.	DEBIT	CREDIT	BALANCE

Income Summary　　　ACCOUNT NO. 901

DATE	ACCOUNT TITLES AND EXPLANATION	P.R.	DEBIT	CREDIT	BALANCE

GENERAL JOURNAL

Date	Account Titles and Explanation	Post Ref.	Debit	Credit

Unadjusted Trial Balance

GENERAL JOURNAL

Date	Account Titles and Explanation	Post Ref.	Debit	Credit

Income Statement

Statement of Changes in Owner's Equity

Balance Sheet

GENERAL JOURNAL

Date	Account Titles and Explanation	Post Ref.	Debit	Credit

Post-Closing Trial Balance

Problem 5-4 or 5-4A

(1)	(6)	(11)	(16)
(2)	(7)	(12)	(17)
(3)	(8)	(13)	(18)
(4)	(9)	(14)	(19)
(5)	(10)	(15)	(20)

No.	Account Title	Unadjusted Trial Balance		Adjustments		Adjusted Trial Balance		Income Statement		Statement of Changes in Owner's Equity and Balance Sheet	
		Dr.	Cr.	Dr.	Cr.	Dr.	Cr.	Dr.	Cr.	Dr.	Cr.

GENERAL JOURNAL

Date	Account Titles and Explanation	Post Ref.	Debit	Credit

GENERAL JOURNAL

Date	Account Titles and Explanation	Post Ref.	Debit	Credit

Income Statement

Statement of Changes in Owner's Equity

Balance Sheet

Current Ratio:

(b)

Title	Unadjusted Trial Balance		Adjustments		Adjusted Trial Balance	

GENERAL JOURNAL

Date	Account Titles and Explanation	Post Ref.	Debit	Credit

GENERAL JOURNAL

Date	Account Titles and Explanation	Post Ref.	Debit	Credit

Part 4

GENERAL JOURNAL

Date	Account Titles and Explanation	Post Ref.	Debit	Credit

GENERAL JOURNAL

Date	Account Titles and Explanation	Post Ref.	Debit	Credit

GENERAL LEDGER

Cash   ACCOUNT NO. 101

DATE	EXPLANATION	P.R.	DEBIT	CREDIT	BALANCE
2000 Dec. 31	Balance				45 245 00

Accounts Receivable   ACCOUNT NO. 106

DATE	EXPLANATION	P.R.	DEBIT	CREDIT	BALANCE
2000 Dec. 31	Balance				2 850 00

Computer Supplies   ACCOUNT NO. 126

DATE	EXPLANATION	P.R.	DEBIT	CREDIT	BALANCE
2000 Dec. 31	Balance				720 00

Prepaid Insurance   ACCOUNT NO. 128

DATE	EXPLANATION	P.R.	DEBIT	CREDIT	BALANCE
2000 Dec. 31	Balance				1 620 00

Prepaid Rent   ACCOUNT NO. 131

DATE	EXPLANATION	P.R.	DEBIT	CREDIT	BALANCE
2000 Dec. 31	Balance				1 125 00

Office Equipment   ACCOUNT NO. 163

DATE	EXPLANATION	P.R.	DEBIT	CREDIT	BALANCE
2000 Dec. 31	Balance				9 000 00

Accumulated Depreciation, Office Equipment   ACCOUNT NO. 164

DATE	EXPLANATION	P.R.	DEBIT	CREDIT	BALANCE
2000 Dec. 31	Balance				750 00

Computer Equipment   ACCOUNT NO. 167

DATE	EXPLANATION	P.R.	DEBIT	CREDIT	BALANCE
2000 Dec. 31	Balance				18 000 00

Accumulated Depreciation, Computer Equipment   ACCOUNT NO. 168

DATE	EXPLANATION	P.R.	DEBIT	CREDIT	BALANCE
2000 Dec. 31	Balance				1 125 00

Accounts Payable   ACCOUNT NO. 201

DATE	EXPLANATION	P.R.	DEBIT	CREDIT	BALANCE
2000 Dec. 31	Balance				1 155 00

Chapter 5   **Serial Problem**
Part 1   **Echo Systems**
          (Continued)

Name _____

Wages Payable   ACCOUNT NO. 210

DATE	EXPLANATION	P.R.	DEBIT	CREDIT	BALANCE
2000 Dec. 31	Balance				400 00

Unearned Computer Services Revenue   ACCOUNT NO. 236

DATE	EXPLANATION	P.R.	DEBIT	CREDIT	BALANCE
2000 Dec. 31	Balance				1 500 00

Mary Graham, Capital   ACCOUNT NO. 301

DATE	EXPLANATION	P.R.	DEBIT	CREDIT	BALANCE
2000 Dec. 31	Balance				72 000 00

Mary Graham, Withdrawals   ACCOUNT NO. 302

DATE	EXPLANATION	P.R.	DEBIT	CREDIT	BALANCE
2000 Dec. 31	Balance				7 200 00

**Chapter 5
Part 1**

**Serial Problem
Echo Systems
(Continued)**

Name _____

Computer Services Revenue   ACCOUNT NO. 403

DATE	EXPLANATION	P.R.	DEBIT	CREDIT	BALANCE
2000 Dec. 31	Balance				26 100 00

Depreciation Expense, Office Equipment   ACCOUNT NO. 612

DATE	EXPLANATION	P.R.	DEBIT	CREDIT	BALANCE
2000 Dec. 31	Balance				750 00

Depreciation Expense, Computer Equipment   ACCOUNT NO. 613

DATE	EXPLANATION	P.R.	DEBIT	CREDIT	BALANCE
2000 Dec. 31	Balance				1 125 00

Wages Expense   ACCOUNT NO. 623

DATE	EXPLANATION	P.R.	DEBIT	CREDIT	BALANCE
2000 Dec. 31	Balance				3 100 00

Insurance Expense   ACCOUNT NO. 637

DATE	EXPLANATION	P.R.	DEBIT	CREDIT	BALANCE
2000 Dec. 31	Balance				540 00

Rent Expense — ACCOUNT NO. 640

DATE	EXPLANATION	P.R.	DEBIT	CREDIT	BALANCE
2000 Dec. 31	Balance				3 375 00

Computer Supplies Expense — ACCOUNT NO. 652

DATE	EXPLANATION	P.R.	DEBIT	CREDIT	BALANCE
2000 Dec. 31	Balance				2 715 00

Advertising Expense — ACCOUNT NO. 655

DATE	EXPLANATION	P.R.	DEBIT	CREDIT	BALANCE
2000 Dec. 31	Balance				2 910 00

Mileage Expense — ACCOUNT NO. 676

DATE	EXPLANATION	P.R.	DEBIT	CREDIT	BALANCE
2000 Dec. 31	Balance				700 00

Chapter 5   **Serial Problem**   *Name*
Part 1   **Echo Systems**
              (Continued)

Miscellaneous Expense   ACCOUNT NO. 677

DATE	EXPLANATION	P.R.	DEBIT	CREDIT	BALANCE
2000 Dec. 31	Balance				750 00

Repairs Expense, Computer   ACCOUNT NO. 684

DATE	EXPLANATION	P.R.	DEBIT	CREDIT	BALANCE
2000 Dec. 31	Balance				1 305 00

Income Summary   ACCOUNT NO. 901

DATE	EXPLANATION	P.R.	DEBIT	CREDIT	BALANCE

Chapter 5
Part 2

Serial Problem
Echo Systems
(Continued)

Name

ECHO SYSTEMS
Post-Closing Trial Balance
December 31, 2000

(1) _____
_____
_____
_____
_____

(2) _____
_____
_____
_____
_____
_____
_____
_____
_____
_____

(3) _____
_____
_____
_____

(4) _____
_____
_____

(5) Swoosh Ahead: _____
_____
_____
_____
_____
_____
_____
_____

(1) _____

_____

_____

_____

_____

_____

_____

_____

_____

(2) _____

_____

_____

_____

_____

(3) _____

_____

_____

_____

(4) _____

_____

_____

_____

_____

(1) _____

_____

_____

_____

_____

_____

_____

_____

_____

_____

_____

_____

_____

_____

_____

_____

_____

(2) _____

_____

_____

_____

_____

_____

_____

_____

_____

_____

_____

_____

_____

_____

_____

_____

_____

MEMORANDUM

TO:

FROM:

SUBJECT:

DATE:

(1) _____

(2) _____

(3) _____

1.

Title	Trial Balance		Adjustments		Balance Sheet	
	Debit	Credit	Debit	Credit	Debit	Credit

2.

Title	Trial Balance		Adjustments		Income Statement	
	Debit	Credit	Debit	Credit	Debit	Credit

GENERAL JOURNAL

Date	Account Titles and Explanation	Post Ref.	Debit	Credit

3.

Title	Trial Balance		Adjustments		Income Statement	
	Debit	Credit	Debit	Credit	Debit	Credit

GENERAL JOURNAL

Date	Account Titles and Explanation	Post Ref.	Debit	Credit

4.

GENERAL JOURNAL

Date	Account Titles and Explanation	Post Ref.	Debit	Credit

5. Proving the Accounting Equation:

(1) _____
_____
_____
_____
_____

(2) _____
_____
_____
_____
_____

(3) _____
_____
_____
_____
_____

(4) _____
_____
_____
_____
_____

(5) _____
_____
_____
_____
_____

(1) _____

(2) _____

(3) _____

(4) _____

(5) _____

(a) _____
(b) _____
(c) _____
(d) _____
(e) _____

Quick Study 6-2

GENERAL JOURNAL

Date	Account Titles and Explanation	Post Ref.	Debit	Credit

GENERAL JOURNAL

Date	Account Titles and Explanation	Post Ref.	Debit	Credit

Quick Study 6-4

GENERAL JOURNAL

Date	Account Titles and Explanation	Post Ref.	Debit	Credit

GENERAL JOURNAL

Date	Account Titles and Explanation	Post Ref.	Debit	Credit

Quick Study 6-6

(a)

(b)

(c) _____
_____
_____
_____
_____
_____

(d) _____
_____
_____
_____
_____

Interpretation of (a) _____
_____
_____

Quick Study 6-7

_____
_____
_____
_____
_____
_____
_____
_____
_____
_____

Quick Study 6-8

_____
_____
_____
_____
_____
_____
_____
_____
_____
_____
_____

(1)	(6)
(2)	(7)
(3)	(8)
(4)	(9)
(5)	(10)

Exercise 6-2

GENERAL JOURNAL

Date	Account Titles and Explanation	Post Ref.	Debit	Credit

GENERAL JOURNAL

Date	Account Titles and Explanation	Post Ref.	Debit	Credit

(b)

GENERAL JOURNAL

Date	Account Titles and Explanation	Post Ref.	Debit	Credit

(a)

GENERAL JOURNAL

Date	Account Titles and Explanation	Post Ref.	Debit	Credit

(b)

GENERAL JOURNAL

Date	Account Titles and Explanation	Post Ref.	Debit	Credit

(c)

_____
_____
_____
_____
_____
_____
_____
_____
_____
_____
_____
_____
_____
_____
_____
_____

Exercise 6-5

	(a)	(b)	(c)
Invoice cost of merchandise purchases			
Purchase discounts received			
Purchase returns and allowances received			
Cost of transportation-in			
Merchandise inventory (beginning of period)			
Total cost of merchandise purchases			
Merchandise inventory (end of period)			
Cost of goods sold			

(a)

(b)

(c)

Exercise 6-8
Entry for Sale of Merchandise

GENERAL JOURNAL

Date	Account Titles and Explanation	Post Ref.	Debit	Credit

Entry for Alternative (a)

GENERAL JOURNAL

Date	Account Titles and Explanation	Post Ref.	Debit	Credit

Entry for Alternative (b)

GENERAL JOURNAL

Date	Account Titles and Explanation	Post Ref.	Debit	Credit

Entry for Alternative (c)

GENERAL JOURNAL

Date	Account Titles and Explanation	Post Ref.	Debit	Credit

Name _____

Entry for Purchase of Merchandise

GENERAL JOURNAL

Date	Account Titles and Explanation	Post Ref.	Debit	Credit

Entry for Alternative (a)

GENERAL JOURNAL

Date	Account Titles and Explanation	Post Ref.	Debit	Credit

Entry for Alternative (b)

GENERAL JOURNAL

Date	Account Titles and Explanation	Post Ref.	Debit	Credit

GENERAL JOURNAL

Date	Account Titles and Explanation	Post Ref.	Debit	Credit

Exercise 6-10

Merchandise Inventory

Cost of Goods Sold

Adjusting Entries:

GENERAL JOURNAL

Date		Account Titles and Explanation	Post Ref.	Debit			Credit		

Closing Entries:

GENERAL JOURNAL

Date	Account Titles and Explanation	Post Ref.	Debit	Credit

Case X

_____
_____
_____
_____
_____
_____

Case Y

_____
_____
_____
_____
_____
_____

Case Z

_____
_____
_____
_____
_____
_____

Best Case:

_____
_____
_____
_____

Exercise 6-13

_____
_____
_____
_____
_____
_____
_____
_____
_____
_____
_____
_____
_____
_____
_____
_____

GENERAL JOURNAL

Date	Account Titles and Explanation	Post Ref.	Debit	Credit

GENERAL JOURNAL

Date	Account Titles and Explanation	Post Ref.	Debit	Credit

Part 1

_____
_____
_____
_____
_____

Part 2

_____
_____
_____
_____
_____

Part 3

_____
_____
_____
_____
_____

GENERAL JOURNAL

Date	Account Titles and Explanation	Post Ref.	Debit	Credit

GENERAL JOURNAL

Date	Account Titles and Explanation	Post Ref.	Debit	Credit

GENERAL JOURNAL

Date	Account Titles and Explanation	Post Ref.	Debit	Credit

GENERAL JOURNAL

Date	Account Titles and Explanation	Post Ref.	Debit	Credit

_____
_____
_____
_____
_____
_____
_____
_____
_____
_____

Part 2

_____
_____
_____
_____
_____
_____
_____
_____
_____
_____
_____

_____

_____

_____

Part 5

_____

_____

_____

_____

_____

_____

GENERAL JOURNAL

Date	Account Titles and Explanation	Post Ref.	Debit	Credit

Part 3

GENERAL JOURNAL

Date	Account Titles and Explanation	Post Ref.	Debit	Credit

Part 2

		Debit	Credit

Part 4

Chapter 6   **Serial Problem**   *Name*
Part 1   **Echo Systems**
Journal Entries

GENERAL JOURNAL

Date	Account Titles and Explanation	Post Ref.	Debit	Credit

Date	Account Titles and Explanation	Post Ref.	Debit	Credit

Chapter 6   **Serial Problem**   *Name*
Part 1   **Echo Systems**
Journal Entries   **(Continued)**

Date	Account Titles and Explanation	Post Ref.	Debit	Credit

Date	Account Titles and Explanation	Post Ref.	Debit	Credit

Name _____

GENERAL LEDGER

Cash   ACCOUNT NO. 101

DATE	EXPLANATION	P.R.	DEBIT	CREDIT	BALANCE
2000 Dec. 31	Balance				45 2 4 5 00

**Chapter 6
Part 2**

**Serial Problem
Echo Systems
(Continued)**

Name

Accounts Receivable – Alamo Engineering   ACCOUNT NO. 106.1

DATE	EXPLANATION	P.R.	DEBIT	CREDIT	BALANCE

Accounts Receivable – Buckman Services   ACCOUNT NO. 106.2

DATE	EXPLANATION	P.R.	DEBIT	CREDIT	BALANCE

Accounts Receivable – Capital Leasing   ACCOUNT NO. 106.3

DATE	EXPLANATION	P.R.	DEBIT	CREDIT	BALANCE

Accounts Receivable – Decker Co.   ACCOUNT NO. 106.4

DATE	EXPLANATION	P.R.	DEBIT	CREDIT	BALANCE
2000 Dec. 31	Balance				1 3 5 0 00

Name _____

Accounts Receivable – Elite Corporation   ACCOUNT NO. 106.5

DATE	EXPLANATION	P.R.	DEBIT	CREDIT	BALANCE

Accounts Receivable – Fostek Co.   ACCOUNT NO. 106.6

DATE	EXPLANATION	P.R.	DEBIT	CREDIT	BALANCE
2000 Dec. 31	Balance				1,5 0 0 00

Accounts Receivable – Grandview Co.   ACCOUNT NO. 106.7

DATE	EXPLANATION	P.R.	DEBIT	CREDIT	BALANCE

Accounts Receivable – Hacienda, Inc.   ACCOUNT NO. 106.8

DATE	EXPLANATION	P.R.	DEBIT	CREDIT	BALANCE

**Chapter 6
Part 2**

**Serial Problem
Echo Systems
(Continued)**

Name

Accounts Receivable – Images, Inc. ACCOUNT NO. 106.9

DATE	EXPLANATION	P.R.	DEBIT	CREDIT	BALANCE

Merchandise Inventory ACCOUNT NO. 119

DATE	EXPLANATION	P.R.	DEBIT	CREDIT	BALANCE

Computer Supplies ACCOUNT NO. 126

DATE	EXPLANATION	P.R.	DEBIT	CREDIT	BALANCE
2000 Dec. 31	Balance				7 2 0 00

Chapter 6
Part 2

Serial Problem
Echo Systems
(Continued)

Name

Prepaid Insurance   ACCOUNT NO. 128

DATE	EXPLANATION	P.R.	DEBIT	CREDIT	BALANCE
2000 Dec. 31	Balance				1 6 2 0 00

Prepaid Rent   ACCOUNT NO. 131

DATE	EXPLANATION	P.R.	DEBIT	CREDIT	BALANCE
2000 Dec. 31	Balance				1 1 2 5 00

Office Equipment   ACCOUNT NO. 163

DATE	EXPLANATION	P.R.	DEBIT	CREDIT	BALANCE
2000 Dec. 31	Balance				9 0 0 0 00

Accumulated Depreciation, Office Equipment   ACCOUNT NO. 164

DATE	EXPLANATION	P.R.	DEBIT	CREDIT	BALANCE
2000 Dec. 31	Balance				7 5 0 00

**Chapter 6
Part 2**

**Serial Problem
Echo Systems
(Continued)**

Name

Computer Equipment — ACCOUNT NO. 167

DATE	EXPLANATION	P.R.	DEBIT	CREDIT	BALANCE
2000 Dec. 31	Balance				18 0 0 0 00

Accumulated Depreciation, Computer Equipment — ACCOUNT NO. 168

DATE	EXPLANATION	P.R.	DEBIT	CREDIT	BALANCE
2000 Dec. 31	Balance				1 1 2 5 00

Accounts Payable — ACCOUNT NO. 201

DATE	EXPLANATION	P.R.	DEBIT	CREDIT	BALANCE
2000 Dec. 31	Balance				1 1 5 5 00

Wages Payable — ACCOUNT NO. 210

DATE	EXPLANATION	P.R.	DEBIT	CREDIT	BALANCE
2000 Dec. 31	Balance				4 0 0 00

Chapter 6
Part 2

Serial Problem
Echo Systems
(Continued)

Name

Unearned Computer Services Revenue ACCOUNT NO. 236

DATE	EXPLANATION	P.R.	DEBIT	CREDIT	BALANCE
2000 Dec. 31	Balance				1 5 0 0 00

Mary Graham, Capital ACCOUNT NO. 301

DATE	EXPLANATION	P.R.	DEBIT	CREDIT	BALANCE
2000 Dec. 31	Balance				73 6 3 0 00

Mary Graham, Withdrawals ACCOUNT NO. 302

DATE	EXPLANATION	P.R.	DEBIT	CREDIT	BALANCE

Computer Services Revenue ACCOUNT NO. 403

DATE	EXPLANATION	P.R.	DEBIT	CREDIT	BALANCE

Sales   ACCOUNT NO. 413

DATE	EXPLANATION	P.R.	DEBIT	CREDIT	BALANCE

Sales Returns and Allowances   ACCOUNT NO. 414

DATE	EXPLANATION	P.R.	DEBIT	CREDIT	BALANCE

Sales Discounts   ACCOUNT NO. 415

DATE	EXPLANATION	P.R.	DEBIT	CREDIT	BALANCE

Cost of Goods Sold   ACCOUNT NO. 502

DATE	EXPLANATION	P.R.	DEBIT	CREDIT	BALANCE

**Chapter 6
Part 2**

**Serial Problem
Echo Systems
(Continued)**

Name

Depreciation Expense, Office Equipment — ACCOUNT NO. 612

DATE	EXPLANATION	P.R.	DEBIT	CREDIT	BALANCE

Depreciation Expense, Computer Equipment — ACCOUNT NO. 613

DATE	EXPLANATION	P.R.	DEBIT	CREDIT	BALANCE

Wages Expense — ACCOUNT NO. 623

DATE	EXPLANATION	P.R.	DEBIT	CREDIT	BALANCE

Insurance Expense — ACCOUNT NO. 637

DATE	EXPLANATION	P.R.	DEBIT	CREDIT	BALANCE

Rent Expense — ACCOUNT NO. 640

DATE	EXPLANATION	P.R.	DEBIT	CREDIT	BALANCE

Computer Supplies Expense   ACCOUNT NO. 652

DATE	EXPLANATION	P.R.	DEBIT	CREDIT	BALANCE

Advertising Expense   ACCOUNT NO. 655

DATE	EXPLANATION	P.R.	DEBIT	CREDIT	BALANCE

Mileage Expense   ACCOUNT NO. 676

DATE	EXPLANATION	P.R.	DEBIT	CREDIT	BALANCE

Miscellaneous Expense   ACCOUNT NO. 677

DATE	EXPLANATION	P.R.	DEBIT	CREDIT	BALANCE

Repairs Expense, Computer   ACCOUNT NO. 684

DATE	EXPLANATION	P.R.	DEBIT	CREDIT	BALANCE

Chapter 6
Part 3

Serial Problem
Echo Systems
(Continued)

Name _____

ECHO SYSTEMS
Partial Work Sheet
March 31, 2001

Acct. No.	Account Title	Unadjusted Trial Balance		Adjustments		Adjusted Trial Balance	
		Dr.	Cr.	Dr.	Cr.	Dr.	Cr.

Chapter 6
Part 4

Serial Problem
Echo Systems
(Continued)

Name _____

ECHO SYSTEMS
Income Statement
For Three Months Ended March 31, 2001

ECHO SYSTEMS

Statement of Changes in Owner's Equity

For Three Months Ended March 31, 2001

Chapter 6
Part 6

Serial Problem
Echo Systems
(Continued)

Name _____

ECHO SYSTEMS
Balance Sheet
March 31, 2001

_____
_____
_____
_____
_____
_____
_____
_____
_____

Part 2

_____
_____
_____
_____
_____
_____
_____
_____
_____
_____
_____
_____
_____
_____
_____

Part 3
Swoosh Ahead: _____
_____
_____
_____
_____
_____
_____
_____
_____
_____
_____

_____
_____
_____
_____
_____
_____
_____
_____
_____
_____
_____
_____
_____
_____
_____
_____
_____
_____

Part 2

_____
_____
_____
_____
_____
_____
_____

Part 3

_____
_____
_____
_____
_____
_____
_____

_____
_____
_____
_____
_____
_____
_____
_____
_____
_____
_____
_____
_____
_____

Part 2

_____
_____
_____
_____
_____
_____
_____
_____
_____

MEMORANDUM

TO:

FROM:

SUBJECT:

DATE:

(1) _____

(2) _____

(3) _____

(4) _____

(5) _____

(6) _____

(7) _____

(8) _____

(9) _____

(10) _____

Teamwork in Action
(1a)

_____

_____

_____

_____

_____

_____

_____

_____

_____

_____

_____
_____
_____
_____
_____
_____
_____
_____
_____
_____

(1c)

_____
_____
_____
_____
_____
_____
_____
_____
_____
_____
_____
_____
_____

(1d)

_____
_____
_____
_____
_____
_____
_____
_____
_____
_____
_____
_____

(2)

Check: Net income is _____.

(3)

Store: _____
_____

Store policy on returns: _____
_____
_____
_____
_____
_____
_____
_____
_____

Sales allowances negotiated: _____
_____
_____
_____
_____
_____
_____
_____
_____

Customer abuses and management actions: _____
_____
_____
_____
_____
_____
_____
_____
_____
_____
_____
_____
_____
_____
_____
_____

(1) _____

_____

_____

_____

_____

_____

(2) _____

_____

_____

_____

_____

_____

(3) _____

_____

_____

_____

_____

_____

(4) _____

_____

_____

_____

_____

_____

(5) _____

_____

_____

_____

_____

_____

_____

(1)

(2)

Quick Study 7-2

Quick Study 7-3

Quick Study 7-4

Quick Study 7-5

(a) FIFO

Date	Purchases	Cost of Goods Sold	Inventory Balance

(b) LIFO

Date	Purchases	Cost of Goods Sold	Inventory Balance

(c) Weighted Average

Date	Purchases	Cost of Goods Sold	Inventory Balance

Quick Study 7-7

(a) _____

(b) _____

(c) _____

(d) _____

(e) _____

(a) _____

_____

(b) _____

_____

(c) _____

_____

(d) _____

_____

(e) _____

_____

(f) _____

_____

_____

Quick Study 7-9

Inventory Items	Units on Hand	Per Unit		Total Cost	Total Market	LCM applied to:	
		Cost	Market			Items	Whole

_____
_____
_____
_____
_____
_____
_____
_____
_____

Exercise 7-1

(a) FIFO Perpetual Inventory System

Date	Purchases	Cost of Goods Sold	Inventory Balance

FIFO Gross Margin:

(b) LIFO Perpetual Inventory System

Date	Purchases	Cost of Goods Sold	Inventory Balance

LIFO Gross Margin:

Specific Identification Inventory System
Ending Inventory and Cost of Goods Sold: _____

_____
_____
_____
_____
_____
_____
_____
_____
_____
_____

Gross Margin: _____

_____
_____
_____
_____
_____
_____

(a)
Specific Identification

_____
_____
_____
_____
_____
_____
_____
_____
_____

(b) Weighted Average Perpetual

Date	Purchases	Cost of Goods Sold	Inventory Balance

(c) FIFO Perpetual

Date	Purchases	Cost of Goods Sold	Inventory Balance

(d) LIFO Perpetual

Date	Purchases	Cost of Goods Sold	Inventory Balance

TROUT, INC.				
Income Statements				
For the year ended December 31, 1999				
	Specific Identification	Weighted Average	FIFO	LIFO

(1) _____

(2) _____

(3) _____

	Ending Inventory	Cost of Goods Sold
(a) Specific Identification		

(b) Weighted Average Periodic

(c) FIFO Periodic

(d) LIFO Periodic

Method with Current Tax Advantage:

	Ending Inventory	Cost of Goods Sold
(a) Specific Identification		

_____
_____
_____
_____
_____

(b) Weighted Average Periodic

_____
_____
_____
_____
_____

(c) FIFO Periodic

_____
_____
_____
_____
_____

(d) LIFO Periodic

_____
_____
_____
_____
_____

Method with Current Tax Advantage:

_____
_____

Exercise 7-7

(1) Gross Profit: _____

_____

(2)	2000			2001			2002		
Sales									
Cost of goods sold:									
Beginning inventory									
Cost of Purchases									
Goods avail. For sale									
Ending inventory									
Cost of goods sold									
Gross profit									

Inventory Items	Units on Hand	Cost	Market	Total Cost	Total Market	Products	Whole

(a) LCM applied to whole: _____

(b) LCM applied to items: _____

Exercise 7-9

	At Cost	At Retail

Exercise 7-10

(a) Estimated cost of physical inventory: _____

_____

_____

b) Shrinkage at cost and at retail:	At Cost	At Retail

_____
_____
_____
_____
_____
_____
_____
_____
_____
_____
_____
_____
_____
_____
_____

Exercise 7-12

Merchandise Turnover (2001): _____
_____
_____
_____

Merchandise Turnover (2000): _____
_____
_____
_____

Days' Sales in Inventory (2001): _____
_____
_____
_____

Days' Sales in Inventory (2000): _____
_____
_____
_____

Comments: _____
_____
_____
_____

(1) _____

_____

_____

_____

_____

_____

_____

_____

_____

_____

_____

(2) _____

_____

_____

_____

_____

3(a) FIFO Perpetual

Date	Purchase	Cost of Goods Sold	Inventory Balance

3(b) LIFO Perpetual

Date	Purchase	Cost of Goods Sold	Inventory Balance

3(c) Specific Identification

3(d) Weighted Average Perpetual

Date	Purchase	Cost of Goods Sold	Inventory Balance

(4)

	FIFO	LIFO	Specific Identification	Weighted Average

(5) _____

_____
_____
_____
_____
_____
_____
_____
_____

Part 2
(a) FIFO Periodic _____
_____
_____
_____
_____
_____
_____
_____
_____

(b) LIFO Periodic _____
_____
_____
_____
_____
_____
_____
_____
_____

(c) Weighted Average Periodic _____
_____
_____
_____
_____
_____
_____
_____
_____

Comparative Income Statements

	FIFO	LIFO	Weighted Average Cost

Supporting Calculations:

_____
_____
_____
_____
_____
_____
_____
_____

Part 3

_____
_____
_____
_____
_____
_____
_____
_____
_____
_____
_____
_____

Problem 7-4 or 7-4A
Part 1

(a) Cost of Goods Sold:	*1999*	*2000*	*2001*
Reported.................................	_____	_____	_____
Adjustments: 12/31/1999 error	_____	_____	_____
12/31/2000 error	_____	_____	_____
Corrected.................................	_____	_____	_____

(b) Net Income:	*1999*	*2000*	*2001*
Reported.................................	_____	_____	_____
Adjustments: 12/31/1999 error	_____	_____	_____
12/31/2000 error	_____	_____	_____
Corrected.................................	_____	_____	_____

(c) Total Current Assets:	*1999*	*2000*	*2001*
Reported.................................	_____	_____	_____
Adjustments: 12/31/1999 error	_____	_____	_____
12/31/2000 error	_____	_____	_____
Corrected.................................	_____	_____	_____

(d) Owner's Equity:	*1999*	*2000*	*2001*
Reported...			
Adjustments: 12/31/1999 error			
12/31/2000 error			
Corrected..			

Part 2

_____

_____

_____

_____

_____

_____

_____

_____

_____

_____

_____

| Inventory Items | Units on Hand | Per Unit | | Total Cost | Total Market | LCM applied to: | | |
		Cost	Market			Items	Categories	Whole

(a) _____

(b) _____

(c) _____

	At Cost	At Retail

Part 2

	At Cost	At Retail

_____

Reporting in Action

(1) _____

(2) _____

(3) _____

(4)

_____

_____

_____

_____

_____

(5)
Merchandise Turnover:

_____

_____

_____

Days' Sales in Inventory:

_____

_____

_____

_____

(6)
Swoosh Ahead:

_____

_____

_____

_____

_____

_____

_____

_____

_____

_____

_____

_____

_____

_____

_____

_____

_____

_____

_____

_____

_____

_____

(1)
Merchandise Turnover – NIKE: _____
_____
_____
_____
_____

Merchandise Turnover – Reebok: _____
_____
_____
_____
_____
_____

(2)
Days' Sales in Inventory – NIKE: _____
_____
_____
_____
_____

Days' Sales in Inventory – Reebok: _____
_____
_____
_____
_____

(3) Interpretation: _____
_____
_____
_____
_____
_____
_____
_____
_____

(1) _____

_____
_____
_____
_____
_____
_____
_____
_____
_____
_____
_____
_____

(2) _____

_____
_____
_____
_____
_____
_____
_____
_____
_____
_____
_____

MEMORANDUM

TO:

FROM:

SUBJECT:

DATE:

(1) _____

(2) _____

(3) _____

_____

_____

_____

_____

(4) Inventory Turnover: _____

_____

_____

Days' Sales in Inventory: _____

_____

_____

_____

Teamwork in Action

(a) and (b) Concept discussion: _____

_____

_____

_____

_____

_____

_____

_____

_____

_____

_____

_____

(a) and (b) Computation:

Date	Purchases	Cost of Goods Sold	Inventory Balance

(c)

(d)

(e)

<u>Store Name</u>	<u>Merchandise Sold</u>	<u>Bar-Coding</u>	<u>Inventory Method</u>	<u>Other</u>

Business Week Activity

(1) _____

_____

(2) _____

_____

(3) _____

_____

_____

_____

_____

_____

(a) _____
(b) _____
(c) _____
(d) _____
(e) _____
(f) _____
(g) _____

Quick Study 8-2

GENERAL JOURNAL

Date	Account Titles and Explanation	Post Ref.	Debit	Credit

Quick Study 8-3

(a) _____	**(f)** _____
(b) _____	**(g)** _____
(c) _____	**(h)** _____
(d) _____	**(i)** _____
(e) _____	**(j)** _____

Quick Study 8-4

(a) _____
(b) _____
(c) _____
(d) _____

Information Reportable: _____
_____
_____
_____
_____

Quick Study 8-6

(1) _____
(2) _____
(3) _____
(4) _____
(5) _____

Exercise 8-1

Sales Journal				
Date	Account Debited	Invoice Number	PR	Accts. Receivable Dr. Sales Cr.

Cash Receipts Journal

Date	Accounts Credited	Explanation	PR	Cash Dr.	Sales Discount Dr.	Accts. Rec. Cr.	Sales Cr.	Other Accts. Cr.

Exercise 8-3

Purchases Journal

Date	Account	Date of Invoice	Terms	PR	Accts. Payable Cr.	Purchases Dr.	Office Supplies Dr.	Other Accts. Dr.

	Ck.		Account		Cash	Purchases Discounts	Other Accts.	Accts. Payable
Date	No.	Payee	Debited	PR	Cr.	Cr.	Dr.	Dr.

Cash Disbursements Journal

Exercise 8-5

_____

_____

_____

_____

_____

_____

_____

ACCOUNTS RECEIVABLE SUBSIDIARY LEDGER

Sanders Farrell	Don Holland	Brad Smithers

Part 2

GENERAL LEDGER

Accounts Receivable	Sales	Sales Returns and Allowances

Part 3

GENERAL LEDGER

Cash	Accounts Payable	Sales Discounts

Accts. Receivable	Notes Payable	Purchases

Prepaid Insurance	Sales	Purchase Returns and Allowances

Store Equipment	Sales Returns and Allowances	Purchase Discounts

ACCOUNTS RECEIVABLE LEDGER

Jack Hertz	Trudy Stone	Dave Waylon

ACCOUNTS PAYABLE LEDGER

Grass Corp.	McGrew Company	Sulter, Inc.

SALES JOURNAL

PURCHASES JOURNAL

CASH RECEIPTS JOURNAL

CASH DISBURSEMENTS JOURNAL

ACCOUNTS RECEIVABLE LEDGER

Adrian Carr	Lisa Mack

Jay Newton	Kathy Olivas

Part 2

GENERAL JOURNAL

Date	Account Titles and Explanation	Post Ref.	Debit	Credit

Part 3

GENERAL LEDGER

Accounts Receivable	Sales

_____

Exercise 8-9

(a) _____

(b) _____

(c) _____

(d) _____

(e) _____

Gen X Sports Company Segment Contribution Matrix for Sales					
Segment	Sales Contribution (in $ mil.)		Sales Contribution (in %)		1-Year Growth Rate Percent
	1999	1998	1999	1998	

Analysis and Interpretation: _____

_____

_____

_____

_____

_____

_____

_____

_____

Sales Journal				Page 3
Date	Account Debited	Invoice Number	PR	Accts. Receivable Dr. Sales Cr.

Cash Receipts Journal								Page 3
Date	Accounts Credited	Explanation	PR	Cash Dr.	Sales Discount Dr.	Accts. Rec. Cr.	Sales Cr.	Other Accts. Cr.

GENERAL LEDGER

Cash   ACCOUNT NO. 101

DATE	EXPLANATION	P.R.	DEBIT	CREDIT	BALANCE

Accounts Receivables   ACCOUNT NO. 106

DATE	EXPLANATION	P.R.	DEBIT	CREDIT	BALANCE

Long-Term Notes Payable   ACCOUNT NO. 251

DATE	EXPLANATION	P.R.	DEBIT	CREDIT	BALANCE

Sales   ACCOUNT NO. 413

DATE	EXPLANATION	P.R.	DEBIT	CREDIT	BALANCE

Sales Discounts   ACCOUNT NO. 415

DATE	EXPLANATION	P.R.	DEBIT	CREDIT	BALANCE

ACCOUNTS RECEIVABLE LEDGER

DATE	EXPLANATION	P.R.	DEBIT	CREDIT	BALANCE

DATE	EXPLANATION	P.R.	DEBIT	CREDIT	BALANCE

DATE	EXPLANATION	P.R.	DEBIT	CREDIT	BALANCE

Trial Balance

Schedule of Accounts Receivable

Part 7

GENERAL JOURNAL   Page 3

Date	Account Titles and Explanation	Post Ref.	Debit	Credit

Purchases Journal								Page 3
Date	Account	Date of Invoice	Terms	PR	Accts. Payable Cr.	Purchases Dr.	Office Supplies Dr.	Other Accts. Dr.

						Purchases	Other	Accts.
	Ck.		Account		Cash	Discounts	Accts.	Payable
Date	No.	Payee	Debited	PR	Cr.	Cr.	Dr.	Dr.

Cash Disbursements Journal — Page 3

GENERAL LEDGER

Cash   ACCOUNT NO. 101

DATE	EXPLANATION	P.R.	DEBIT	CREDIT	BALANCE

Office Supplies   ACCOUNT NO. 124

DATE	EXPLANATION	P.R.	DEBIT	CREDIT	BALANCE

Store Supplies   ACCOUNT NO. 125

DATE	EXPLANATION	P.R.	DEBIT	CREDIT	BALANCE

Store Equipment   ACCOUNT NO. 165

DATE	EXPLANATION	P.R.	DEBIT	CREDIT	BALANCE

Accounts Payable   ACCOUNT NO. 201

DATE	EXPLANATION	P.R.	DEBIT	CREDIT	BALANCE

Long-Term Notes Payable   **ACCOUNT NO. 251**

DATE	EXPLANATION	P.R.	DEBIT	CREDIT	BALANCE

Purchases   **ACCOUNT NO. 505**

DATE	EXPLANATION	P.R.	DEBIT	CREDIT	BALANCE

Purchases Returns and Allowances   **ACCOUNT NO. 506**

DATE	EXPLANATION	P.R.	DEBIT	CREDIT	BALANCE

Purchases Discounts   **ACCOUNT NO. 507**

DATE	EXPLANATION	P.R.	DEBIT	CREDIT	BALANCE

Sales Salaries Expense   **ACCOUNT NO. 621**

DATE	EXPLANATION	P.R.	DEBIT	CREDIT	BALANCE

Advertising Expense   **ACCOUNT NO. 655**

DATE	EXPLANATION	P.R.	DEBIT	CREDIT	BALANCE

ACCOUNTS PAYABLE LEDGER

DATE	EXPLANATION	P.R.	DEBIT	CREDIT	BALANCE

DATE	EXPLANATION	P.R.	DEBIT	CREDIT	BALANCE

ACCOUNTS PAYABLE LEDGER

DATE	EXPLANATION	P.R.	DEBIT	CREDIT	BALANCE

DATE	EXPLANATION	P.R.	DEBIT	CREDIT	BALANCE

Part 6

Trial Balance

_____

_____

Schedule of Accounts Payable

Problem 8-3
Part 1

Sales Journal				Page 3
Date	Account Debited	Invoice Number	PR	Accts. Receivable Dr. Sales Cr.
Dec. 6	Marge Craig	913	✓	3,300
12	Vickie Foresman	914	✓	3,650
15	Amy Ihrig	915	✓	3,100

Purchases Journal								Page 2
Date	Account	Date of Inv.	Terms	PR	Accts. Pay. Cr.	Purchases Dr.	Office Supplies Dr.	Other Accts. Dr.
Dec. 2	Shore Co.	12/2	2/10, n/60	✓	3,200	3,200		
5	Brown Supply	12/3	n/10, EOM	✓	1,300	1,300		
15	Shore Co.	12/15	2/10, n/60	✓	3,990	3,990		
15	Sunshine Co.	12/15	2/10, n/60	✓	2,650	2,650		

Cash Receipts Journal								Page 3
Date	Accounts Credited	Explanation	PR	Cash Dr.	Sales Disc. Dr.	Accts. Rec. Cr.	Sales Cr.	Other Accts. Cr.
Dec. 2	Bill Grigsby	Inv. 11/23	✓	4,116	84	4,200		
15	Sales	Cash sales	✓	38,830			38,830	
15	Marge Craig	Inv. 12/6	✓	2,401	49	2,450		

Cash Disbursements Journal								Page 4
Date	Ck. No.	Payee	Account Debited	PR	Cash Cr.	Purch. Disc. Cr.	Other Accts. Dr.	Accts. Payable Dr.
Dec. 2	619	Omni Realty Co.	Rent Exp.	640	2,250		2,250	
6	620	Fireside Co.	Fireside Co.	✓	3,724	76		3,800
12	621	Shore Co.	Shore Co.	✓	3,136	64		3,200
15	622	Jamie Green	Sales Salaries Exp.	621	2,020		2,020	

GENERAL JOURNAL

Date		Account Titles and Explanation	Post Ref.	Debit		Credit	
Dec.	4	Accounts Payable—Fireside Company	201/✓	460	00		
		Purchases Returns and Allowances	506			460	00
		Received a credit memo for returns.					
	9	Sales Returns and Allowances	414	850	00		
		Accounts Receivable—Marge Craig	106/✓			850	00
		Issued a credit memorandum.					

Name _____

ACCOUNTS RECEIVABLE LEDGER
Marge Craig

DATE	EXPLANATION	P.R.	DEBIT	CREDIT	BALANCE
Dec. 6		S3	3 3 0 0 00		3 3 0 0 00
9		G2		8 5 0 00	2 4 5 0 00
15		R3		2 4 5 0 00	0 00

Vickie Foresman

DATE	EXPLANATION	P.R.	DEBIT	CREDIT	BALANCE
Dec. 12		S3	3 6 5 0 00		3 6 5 0 00

Bill Grigsby

DATE	EXPLANATION	P.R.	DEBIT	CREDIT	BALANCE
Nov. 23		S2	4 2 0 0 00		4 2 0 0 00
Dec. 2		R3		4 2 0 0 00	0 00

Amy Ihrig

DATE	EXPLANATION	P.R.	DEBIT	CREDIT	BALANCE
Dec. 15		S3	3 1 0 0 00		3 1 0 0 00

ACCOUNTS PAYABLE LEDGER
Fireside Company

DATE	EXPLANATION	P.R.	DEBIT	CREDIT	BALANCE
Nov. 28		P1		4 2 6 0 00	4 2 6 0 00
Dec. 4		G2	4 6 0 00		3 8 0 0 00
6		D4	3 8 0 0 00		0 00

Brown Supply Company

DATE	EXPLANATION	P.R.	DEBIT	CREDIT	BALANCE
Dec. 5		P2		1 3 0 0 00	1 3 0 0 00

Sunshine Company

DATE	EXPLANATION	P.R.	DEBIT	CREDIT	BALANCE
Dec. 15		P2		2 6 5 0 00	2 6 5 0 00

Shore Company

DATE	EXPLANATION	P.R.	DEBIT	CREDIT	BALANCE
Dec. 2		P2		3 2 0 0 00	3 2 0 0 00
12		D4	3 2 0 0 00		0 00
15		P2		3 9 9 0 00	3 9 9 0 00

GENERAL LEDGER

Cash   ACCOUNT NO. 101

DATE	EXPLANATION	P.R.	DEBIT	CREDIT	BALANCE
Nov. 30	Balance				5 3 6 1 00

Accounts Receivable   ACCOUNT NO. 106

DATE	EXPLANATION	P.R.	DEBIT	CREDIT	BALANCE
Nov. 30	Balance				4 2 0 0 00
Dec. 9		G2		8 5 0 00	3 3 5 0 00

Merchandise Inventory   ACCOUNT NO. 119

DATE	EXPLANATION	P.R.	DEBIT	CREDIT	BALANCE
Nov. 30	Balance				66 9 7 0 00

Office Supplies   ACCOUNT NO. 124

DATE	EXPLANATION	P.R.	DEBIT	CREDIT	BALANCE
Nov. 30	Balance				6 0 7 00

Store Supplies   ACCOUNT NO. 125

DATE	EXPLANATION	P.R.	DEBIT	CREDIT	BALANCE
Nov. 30	Balance				3 4 6 00

Store Equipment   ACCOUNT NO. 165

DATE	EXPLANATION	P.R.	DEBIT	CREDIT	BALANCE
Nov. 30	Balance				42 1 2 9 00

Accumulated Depreciation, Store Equipment   ACCOUNT NO. 166

DATE	EXPLANATION	P.R.	DEBIT	CREDIT	BALANCE
Nov. 30	Balance				9 1 5 3 00

Accounts Payable   ACCOUNT NO. 201

DATE	EXPLANATION	P.R.	DEBIT	CREDIT	BALANCE
Nov. 30	Balance				4 2 6 0 00
Dec. 4		G2	4 6 0 00		3 8 0 0 00

Name _____

Ken Shaw, Capital   ACCOUNT NO. 301

DATE	EXPLANATION	P.R.	DEBIT	CREDIT	BALANCE
Nov. 30	Balance				106 2 0 0 00

Ken Shaw, Withdrawals   ACCOUNT NO. 302

DATE	EXPLANATION	P.R.	DEBIT	CREDIT	BALANCE

Sales   ACCOUNT NO. 413

DATE	EXPLANATION	P.R.	DEBIT	CREDIT	BALANCE

Sales Returns and Allowances   ACCOUNT NO. 414

DATE	EXPLANATION	P.R.	DEBIT	CREDIT	BALANCE
Dec. 9		G2	8 5 0 00		8 5 0 00

Sales Discounts   ACCOUNT NO. 415

DATE	EXPLANATION	P.R.	DEBIT	CREDIT	BALANCE

Purchases   ACCOUNT NO. 505

DATE	EXPLANATION	P.R.	DEBIT	CREDIT	BALANCE

Purchases Returns and Allowances — ACCOUNT NO. 506

DATE	EXPLANATION	P.R.	DEBIT	CREDIT	BALANCE
Dec. 4		G2		4 6 0 00	4 6 0 00

Purchases Discounts — ACCOUNT NO. 507

DATE	EXPLANATION	P.R.	DEBIT	CREDIT	BALANCE

Sales Salaries Expense — ACCOUNT NO. 621

DATE	EXPLANATION	P.R.	DEBIT	CREDIT	BALANCE
Dec. 15		D4	2 0 2 0 00		2 0 2 0 00

Rent Expense — ACCOUNT NO. 640

DATE	EXPLANATION	P.R.	DEBIT	CREDIT	BALANCE
Dec. 2		D4	2 2 5 0 00		2 2 5 0 00

Utilities Expense — ACCOUNT NO. 690

DATE	EXPLANATION	P.R.	DEBIT	CREDIT	BALANCE

SASKAN ENTERPRISES
Trial Balance
December 31

SASKAN ENTERPRISES
Schedule of Accounts Receivable
December 31

SASKAN ENTERPRISES
Schedule of Accounts Payable
December 31

Problem 8-3A
Part 1

	Sales Journal			Page 3
Date	**Account Debited**	**Invoice Number**	**PR**	**Accts. Receivable Dr. Sales Cr.**
Dec. 6	Marge Craig	913	✓	3,300
12	Heather Flatt	914	✓	3,650
15	Amy Izon	915	✓	3,100

Purchases Journal   Page 2

Date	Account	Date of Inv.	Terms	PR	Accts. Pay. Cr.	Purchases Dr.	Office Supplies Dr.	Other Accts. Dr.
Dec. 2	Walters Co.	12/2	2/10, n/60	✓	3,200	3,200		
5	Green Supply Co.	12/3	n/10, EOM	✓	1,300	1,300		
15	Walters Co.	12/15	2/10, n/60	✓	3,990	3,990		
15	Sunshine Co.	12/15	2/10, n/60	✓	2,650	2,650		

Cash Receipts Journal   Page 3

Date	Accounts Credited	Explanation	PR	Cash Dr.	Sales Disc. Dr.	Accts. Rec. Cr.	Sales Cr.	Other Accts. Cr.
Dec. 2	Jan Wildman	Inv. 11/23	✓	4,116	84	4,200		
15	Sales	Cash sales	✓	38,830			38,830	
15	Marge Craig	Inv. 12/6	✓	2,401	49	2,450		

Cash Disbursements Journal   Page 4

Date	Ck. No.	Payee	Account Debited	PR	Cash Cr.	Purch. Disc. Cr.	Other Accts. Dr.	Accts. Payable Dr.
Dec. 2	619	Omni Realty Co.	Rent Exp.	640	2,250		2,250	
6	620	Fireside Co.	Fireside Co.	✓	3,724	76		3,800
12	621	Walters Co.	Walters Co.	✓	3,136	64		3,200
15	622	Jamie Ford	Sales Salaries Exp.	621	2,620		2,620	

Name _____

GENERAL JOURNAL

Date		Account Titles and Explanation	Post Ref.	Debit			Credit		
Dec.	4	Accounts Payable—Fireside Company	201/✓	460	00				
		Purchases Returns and Allowances	506				460	00	
		Received a credit memo for returns.							
	9	Sales Returns and Allowances	414	850	00				
		Accounts Receivable—Marge Craig	106/✓				850	00	
		Issued a credit memorandum.							

ACCOUNTS RECEIVABLE LEDGER

Marge Craig

DATE	EXPLANATION	P.R.	DEBIT	CREDIT	BALANCE
Dec. 6		S3	3 3 0 0 00		3 3 0 0 00
9		G2		8 5 0 00	2 4 5 0 00
15		R3		2 4 5 0 00	0 00

Heather Flatt

DATE	EXPLANATION	P.R.	DEBIT	CREDIT	BALANCE
Dec. 12		S3	3 6 5 0 00		3 6 5 0 00

Amy Izon

DATE	EXPLANATION	P.R.	DEBIT	CREDIT	BALANCE
Dec. 15		S3	3 1 0 0 00		3 1 0 0 00

Jan Wildman

DATE	EXPLANATION	P.R.	DEBIT	CREDIT	BALANCE
Nov. 23		S2	4 2 0 0 00		4 2 0 0 00
Dec. 2		R3		4 2 0 0 00	0 00

ACCOUNTS PAYABLE LEDGER

Fireside Company

DATE	EXPLANATION	P.R.	DEBIT	CREDIT	BALANCE
Nov. 28		P1		4 2 6 0 00	4 2 6 0 00
Dec. 4		G2	4 6 0 00		3 8 0 0 00
6		D4	3 8 0 0 00		0 00

Green Supply Company

DATE	EXPLANATION	P.R.	DEBIT	CREDIT	BALANCE
Dec. 5		P2		1 3 0 0 00	1 3 0 0 00

Sunshine Company

DATE	EXPLANATION	P.R.	DEBIT	CREDIT	BALANCE
Dec. 15		P2		2 6 5 0 00	2 6 5 0 00

Walters Company

DATE	EXPLANATION	P.R.	DEBIT	CREDIT	BALANCE
Dec. 2		P2		3 2 0 0 00	3 2 0 0 00
12		D4	3 2 0 0 00		0 00
15		P2		3 9 9 0 00	3 9 9 0 00

GENERAL LEDGER

Cash   ACCOUNT NO. 101

DATE	EXPLANATION	P.R.	DEBIT	CREDIT	BALANCE
Nov. 30	Balance				5 3 6 1 00

Accounts Receivable   ACCOUNT NO. 106

DATE	EXPLANATION	P.R.	DEBIT	CREDIT	BALANCE
Nov. 30	Balance				4 2 0 0 00
Dec. 9		G2		8 5 0 00	3 3 5 0 00

Merchandise Inventory   ACCOUNT NO. 119

DATE	EXPLANATION	P.R.	DEBIT	CREDIT	BALANCE
Nov. 30	Balance				66 9 7 0 00

Office Supplies   ACCOUNT NO. 124

DATE		EXPLANATION	P.R.	DEBIT	CREDIT	BALANCE
Nov.	30	Balance				6 0 7 00

Store Supplies   ACCOUNT NO. 125

DATE		EXPLANATION	P.R.	DEBIT	CREDIT	BALANCE
Nov.	30	Balance				3 4 6 00

Store Equipment   ACCOUNT NO. 165

DATE		EXPLANATION	P.R.	DEBIT	CREDIT	BALANCE
Nov.	30	Balance				42 1 2 9 00

Accumulated Depreciation, Store Equipment   ACCOUNT NO. 166

DATE		EXPLANATION	P.R.	DEBIT	CREDIT	BALANCE
Nov.	30	Balance				9 1 5 3 00

Accounts Payable   ACCOUNT NO. 201

DATE		EXPLANATION	P.R.	DEBIT	CREDIT	BALANCE
Nov.	30	Balance				4 2 6 0 00
Dec.	4		G2	4 6 0 00		3 8 0 0 00

Marlee Levin, Capital   ACCOUNT NO. 301

DATE	EXPLANATION	P.R.	DEBIT	CREDIT	BALANCE
Nov. 30	Balance				106 2 0 0 00

Marlee Levin, Withdrawals   ACCOUNT NO. 302

DATE	EXPLANATION	P.R.	DEBIT	CREDIT	BALANCE

Sales   ACCOUNT NO. 413

DATE	EXPLANATION	P.R.	DEBIT	CREDIT	BALANCE

Sales Returns and Allowances   ACCOUNT NO. 414

DATE	EXPLANATION	P.R.	DEBIT	CREDIT	BALANCE
Dec. 9		G2	8 5 0 00		8 5 0 00

Sales Discounts   ACCOUNT NO. 415

DATE	EXPLANATION	P.R.	DEBIT	CREDIT	BALANCE

Purchases   ACCOUNT NO. 505

DATE	EXPLANATION	P.R.	DEBIT	CREDIT	BALANCE

Purchases Returns and Allowances   ACCOUNT NO. 506

DATE	EXPLANATION	P.R.	DEBIT	CREDIT	BALANCE
Dec. 4		G2		4 6 0 00	4 6 0 00

Purchases Discounts   ACCOUNT NO. 507

DATE	EXPLANATION	P.R.	DEBIT	CREDIT	BALANCE

Sales Salaries Expense   ACCOUNT NO. 621

DATE	EXPLANATION	P.R.	DEBIT	CREDIT	BALANCE
Dec. 15		D4	2 6 2 0 00		2 6 2 0 00

Rent Expense   ACCOUNT NO. 640

DATE	EXPLANATION	P.R.	DEBIT	CREDIT	BALANCE
Dec. 2		D4	2 2 5 0 00		2 2 5 0 00

Utilities Expense   ACCOUNT NO. 690

DATE	EXPLANATION	P.R.	DEBIT	CREDIT	BALANCE

Fundamental Accounting Principles, 15th Edition

STARSHINE PRODUCTS
Trial Balance
December 31

STARSHINE PRODUCTS
Schedule of Accounts Receivable
December 31

STARSHINE PRODUCTS
Schedule of Accounts Payable
December 31

Problem 8-4 or 8-4A
Parts 1 and 2

Sales Journal				Page 2
Date	Account Debited	Invoice Number	PR	Accts. Receivable Dr. Sales Cr.

Cash Receipts Journal								Page 2
Date	Accounts Credited	Explanation	PR	Cash Dr.	Sales Disc. Dr.	Accts. Rec. Cr.	Sales Cr.	Other Accts. Cr.

| | | Purchases Journal | | | | | | Page 2 |
Date	Account	Date of Inv.	Terms	PR	Accts. Pay. Cr.	Purchases Dr.	Office Supplies Dr.	Other Accts. Dr.

| | | | Cash Disbursements Journal | | | | | | Page 2 |
Date	Ck. No.	Payee	Account Debited	PR	Cash Cr.	Purch. Disc. Cr.	Other Accts. Dr.	Accts. Payable Dr.

GENERAL JOURNAL

Date	Account Titles and Explanation	Post Ref.	Debit	Credit

GENERAL LEDGER

Cash   ACCOUNT NO. 101

DATE	EXPLANATION	P.R.	DEBIT	CREDIT	BALANCE

Accounts Receivable   ACCOUNT NO. 106

DATE	EXPLANATION	P.R.	DEBIT	CREDIT	BALANCE

Office Supplies   ACCOUNT NO. 124

DATE	EXPLANATION	P.R.	DEBIT	CREDIT	BALANCE

Store Supplies   ACCOUNT NO. 125

DATE	EXPLANATION	P.R.	DEBIT	CREDIT	BALANCE

Office Equipment   ACCOUNT NO. 163

DATE	EXPLANATION	P.R.	DEBIT	CREDIT	BALANCE

Accounts Payable   ACCOUNT NO. 201

DATE	EXPLANATION	P.R.	DEBIT	CREDIT	BALANCE

Long-Term Notes Payable — ACCOUNT NO. 251

DATE	EXPLANATION	P.R.	DEBIT	CREDIT	BALANCE

Sales — ACCOUNT NO. 413

DATE	EXPLANATION	P.R.	DEBIT	CREDIT	BALANCE

Sales Discounts — ACCOUNT NO. 415

DATE	EXPLANATION	P.R.	DEBIT	CREDIT	BALANCE

Purchases — ACCOUNT NO. 505

DATE	EXPLANATION	P.R.	DEBIT	CREDIT	BALANCE

Purchases Returns and Allowances — ACCOUNT NO. 506

DATE	EXPLANATION	P.R.	DEBIT	CREDIT	BALANCE

Purchases Discounts — ACCOUNT NO. 507

DATE	EXPLANATION	P.R.	DEBIT	CREDIT	BALANCE

Sales Salaries Expense   ACCOUNT NO. 621

DATE	EXPLANATION	P.R.	DEBIT	CREDIT	BALANCE

ACCOUNTS RECEIVABLE LEDGER

DATE	EXPLANATION	P.R.	DEBIT	CREDIT	BALANCE

DATE	EXPLANATION	P.R.	DEBIT	CREDIT	BALANCE

DATE	EXPLANATION	P.R.	DEBIT	CREDIT	BALANCE

ACCOUNTS PAYABLE LEDGER

_____

DATE	EXPLANATION	P.R.	DEBIT	CREDIT	BALANCE

_____

DATE	EXPLANATION	P.R.	DEBIT	CREDIT	BALANCE

_____

DATE	EXPLANATION	P.R.	DEBIT	CREDIT	BALANCE

_____

DATE	EXPLANATION	P.R.	DEBIT	CREDIT	BALANCE

Trial Balance

Schedule of Accounts Receivable

Schedule of Accounts Payable

Name _____

Sales Journal   Page 2

Date	Account Debited	Invoice Number	PR	Accts. Receivable Dr. Sales Cr.

Purchases Journal

Date	Account	Date of Inv.	Terms	PR	Accts. Pay. Cr.	Purchases Dr.	Office Supplies Dr.	Other Accts. Dr.

					Cash Receipts Journal				Page 2
Date	Accounts Credited	Explanation	PR	Cash Dr.	Sales Disc. Dr.	Accts. Rec. Cr.	Sales Cr.	Other Accts. Cr.

					Cash Disbursements Journal				Page 2
Date	Ck. No.	Payee	Account Debited	PR	Cash Cr.	Purch. Disc. Cr.	Other Accts. Dr.	Accts. Payable Dr.

GENERAL JOURNAL   Page 3

Date	Account Titles and Explanation	Post Ref.	Debit	Credit

Date	Account Titles and Explanation	Post Ref.	Debit	Credit

GENERAL LEDGER

Cash   ACCOUNT NO. 101

DATE	EXPLANATION	P.R.	DEBIT	CREDIT	BALANCE
Apr. 30	Balance	✓			50 2 4 7 00

Accounts Receivable   ACCOUNT NO. 106

DATE	EXPLANATION	P.R.	DEBIT	CREDIT	BALANCE
Apr. 30	Balance	✓			4 7 2 5 00

Merchandise Inventory   ACCOUNT NO. 119

DATE	EXPLANATION	P.R.	DEBIT	CREDIT	BALANCE
Apr. 30	Balance	✓			220 0 8 0 00

Office Supplies   ACCOUNT NO. 124

DATE	EXPLANATION	P.R.	DEBIT	CREDIT	BALANCE
Apr. 30	Balance	✓			4 3 0 00

Store Supplies   ACCOUNT NO. 125

DATE	EXPLANATION	P.R.	DEBIT	CREDIT	BALANCE
Apr. 30	Balance	✓			2 4 4 7 00

Prepaid Insurance   ACCOUNT NO. 128

DATE	EXPLANATION	P.R.	DEBIT	CREDIT	BALANCE
Apr. 30	Balance	✓			3 3 1 8 00

Office Equipment   ACCOUNT NO. 163

DATE	EXPLANATION	P.R.	DEBIT	CREDIT	BALANCE
Apr. 30	Balance	✓			22 4 7 0 00

Accumulated Depreciation, Office Equipment   ACCOUNT NO. 164

DATE	EXPLANATION	P.R.	DEBIT	CREDIT	BALANCE
Apr. 30	Balance	✓			9 8 9 8 00

Store Equipment   ACCOUNT NO. 165

DATE	EXPLANATION	P.R.	DEBIT	CREDIT	BALANCE
Apr. 30	Balance	✓			38 9 2 0 00

Accumulated Depreciation, Store Equipment   ACCOUNT NO. 166

DATE	EXPLANATION	P.R.	DEBIT	CREDIT	BALANCE
Apr. 30	Balance	✓			17 5 5 6 00

Accounts Payable   ACCOUNT NO. 201

DATE		EXPLANATION	P.R.	DEBIT	CREDIT	BALANCE
Apr.	30	Balance	✓			7 0 9 8 00

Clint Barry, capital   ACCOUNT NO. 301

DATE		EXPLANATION	P.R.	DEBIT	CREDIT	BALANCE
Apr.	30	Balance	✓			308 0 8 5 00

Clint Barry, withdrawals   ACCOUNT NO. 302

DATE	EXPLANATION	P.R.	DEBIT	CREDIT	BALANCE

Sales   ACCOUNT NO. 413

DATE	EXPLANATION	P.R.	DEBIT	CREDIT	BALANCE

Sales Returns and Allowances   ACCOUNT NO. 414

DATE	EXPLANATION	P.R.	DEBIT	CREDIT	BALANCE

Sales Discounts   ACCOUNT NO. 415

DATE	EXPLANATION	P.R.	DEBIT	CREDIT	BALANCE

Purchases   ACCOUNT NO. 505

DATE	EXPLANATION	P.R.	DEBIT	CREDIT	BALANCE

Purchases Returns and Allowances   ACCOUNT NO. 506

DATE	EXPLANATION	P.R.	DEBIT	CREDIT	BALANCE

Purchases Discounts   ACCOUNT NO. 507

DATE	EXPLANATION	P.R.	DEBIT	CREDIT	BALANCE

Depreciation Expense, Office Equipment   ACCOUNT NO. 612

DATE	EXPLANATION	P.R.	DEBIT	CREDIT	BALANCE

Depreciation Expense, Store Equipment   ACCOUNT NO. 613

DATE	EXPLANATION	P.R.	DEBIT	CREDIT	BALANCE

Office Salaries Expense   ACCOUNT NO. 620

DATE	EXPLANATION	P.R.	DEBIT	CREDIT	BALANCE

Sales Salaries Expense   ACCOUNT NO. 621

DATE	EXPLANATION	P.R.	DEBIT	CREDIT	BALANCE

Insurance Expense   ACCOUNT NO. 637

DATE	EXPLANATION	P.R.	DEBIT	CREDIT	BALANCE

Rent Expense, Office Space   ACCOUNT NO. 641

DATE	EXPLANATION	P.R.	DEBIT	CREDIT	BALANCE

Rent Expense, Selling Space   ACCOUNT NO. 642

DATE	EXPLANATION	P.R.	DEBIT	CREDIT	BALANCE

Office Supplies Expense   ACCOUNT NO. 650

DATE	EXPLANATION	P.R.	DEBIT	CREDIT	BALANCE

Store Supplies Expense
ACCOUNT NO. 651

DATE	EXPLANATION	P.R.	DEBIT	CREDIT	BALANCE

Utilities Expense
ACCOUNT NO. 690

DATE	EXPLANATION	P.R.	DEBIT	CREDIT	BALANCE

Income Summary
ACCOUNT NO. 901

DATE	EXPLANATION	P.R.	DEBIT	CREDIT	BALANCE

ACCOUNTS RECEIVABLE LEDGER

NAME   Deaver Corp.

DATE	EXPLANATION	P.R.	DEBIT	CREDIT	BALANCE

NAME   Essex Company

DATE	EXPLANATION	P.R.	DEBIT	CREDIT	BALANCE

NAME Nabors, Inc. _____

DATE	EXPLANATION	P.R.	DEBIT	CREDIT	BALANCE
Apr. 28		S2	4 7 2 5 00		4 7 2 5 00

NAME Oscar Services. _____

DATE	EXPLANATION	P.R.	DEBIT	CREDIT	BALANCE

ACCOUNTS PAYABLE LEDGER

NAME Chandler Corp. _____

DATE	EXPLANATION	P.R.	DEBIT	CREDIT	BALANCE

NAME Gale, Inc. _____

DATE	EXPLANATION	P.R.	DEBIT	CREDIT	BALANCE

NAME   Parkay Products

DATE	EXPLANATION	P.R.	DEBIT	CREDIT	BALANCE
Apr. 29		P2		7 0 9 8 00	7 0 9 8 00

NAME   Thompson Supply Co.

DATE	EXPLANATION	P.R.	DEBIT	CREDIT	BALANCE

Alpine Company
Work Sheet
For Month Ended May 31, 2000

Account Titles	Trial Balance		Adjustments		Income Statement		Statement of Changes in Owner's Equity and Balance Sheet	
	Dr.	Cr.	Dr.	Cr.	Dr.	Cr.	Dr.	Cr.

Alpine Company
Income Statement
For Month Ended May 31, 2000

Alpine Company
Statement of Changes in Owner's Equity
For Month Ended May 31, 2000

Alpine Company
Balance Sheet
May 31, 2000

Alpine Company
Post-Closing Trial Balance
May 31, 2000

Alpine Company
Schedule of Accounts Receivable
May 31, 2000

Alpine Company
Schedule of Accounts Payable
May 31, 2000

(1) _____
_____

(2) Segment Contribution for Revenue

Segment	Revenue Contribution ($)	Revenue Contribution (%)

Segment Contribution for Operating Income

Segment	Operating Income Contribution ($)	Operating Income Contribution (%)

(3) Segment Contribution for Operating Income (1996-1997)

Segment	Operating Income Contribution ($) May 31, 1997	May 31, 1996	1-Year Growth Rate %

(4) Swoosh Ahead:

Segment	Revenue Contribution ($)	Revenue Contribution (%)

Segment	Operating Income Contribution ($)	Operating Income Contribution (%)

Segment	Operating Income Contribution ($)		Growth Rate (%)

NIKE Segment Contribution for Revenue

Segment	Revenue Contribution ($)		1-Year Growth Rate (%)
	May 31, 1997	May 31, 1996	

Reebok Segment Contribution for Net Sales

Segment	Revenue Contribution ($)		1-Year Growth Rate (%)
	Dec. 31, 1996	Dec. 31, 1995	

Part 1 Interpretation: _____

_____

Part 2 Interpretation: _____

_____

_____

Part 3 Growth Analysis: _____

_____

_____

_____

(1) _____

_____

_____

_____

_____

_____

_____

(2) _____

_____

_____

_____

_____

_____

_____

_____

_____

_____

_____

_____

_____

(3) _____

_____

_____

_____

_____

_____

_____

_____

_____

_____

_____

_____

_____

_____

MEMORANDUM

TO:

FROM:

SUBJECT:

DATE:

(1) Contents

_____
_____
_____
_____
_____
_____
_____
_____
_____
_____
_____
_____
_____
_____
_____
_____
_____
_____

(2) Agenda:

_____
_____
_____
_____
_____
_____
_____
_____
_____
_____
_____
_____
_____
_____

Sales Journal				Page 2
Date	**Account Debited**	**Invoice Number**	**PR**	**Accts. Receivable Dr. Sales Cr.**

Cash Receipts Journal								Page 2
Date	**Accounts Credited**	**Explanation**	**PR**	**Cash Dr.**	**Sales Disc. Dr.**	**Accts. Rec. Cr.**	**Sales Cr.**	**Other Accts. Cr.**

| | | | | | | Purchases Journal | | | Page 2 |
Date	Account	Date of Inv.	Terms	PR	Accts. Pay. Cr.	Purchases Dr.	Office Supplies Dr.	Other Accts. Dr.

| | | | | Cash Disbursements Journal | | | | | Page 2 |
Date	Ck. No.	Payee	Account Debited	PR	Cash Cr.	Purch. Disc. Cr.	Other Accts. Dr.	Accts. Payable Dr.

GENERAL JOURNAL

Date	Account Titles and Explanation	Post Ref.	Debit	Credit

GENERAL LEDGER

Cash   ACCOUNT NO. 101

DATE	EXPLANATION	P.R.	DEBIT	CREDIT	BALANCE

Accounts Receivable   ACCOUNT NO. 106

DATE	EXPLANATION	P.R.	DEBIT	CREDIT	BALANCE

Office Supplies   ACCOUNT NO. 124

DATE	EXPLANATION	P.R.	DEBIT	CREDIT	BALANCE

Store Supplies   ACCOUNT NO. 125

DATE	EXPLANATION	P.R.	DEBIT	CREDIT	BALANCE

Office Equipment   ACCOUNT NO. 163

DATE	EXPLANATION	P.R.	DEBIT	CREDIT	BALANCE

Accounts Payable   ACCOUNT NO. 201

DATE	EXPLANATION	P.R.	DEBIT	CREDIT	BALANCE

Long-Term Notes Payable   ACCOUNT NO. 251

DATE	EXPLANATION	P.R.	DEBIT	CREDIT	BALANCE

Sales   ACCOUNT NO. 413

DATE	EXPLANATION	P.R.	DEBIT	CREDIT	BALANCE

Sales Discounts   ACCOUNT NO. 415

DATE	EXPLANATION	P.R.	DEBIT	CREDIT	BALANCE

Purchases   ACCOUNT NO. 505

DATE	EXPLANATION	P.R.	DEBIT	CREDIT	BALANCE

Purchases Discounts   ACCOUNT NO. 507

DATE	EXPLANATION	P.R.	DEBIT	CREDIT	BALANCE

Sales Salaries Expense   ACCOUNT NO. 621

DATE	EXPLANATION	P.R.	DEBIT	CREDIT	BALANCE

ACCOUNTS RECEIVABLE LEDGER

DATE	EXPLANATION	P.R.	DEBIT	CREDIT	BALANCE

DATE	EXPLANATION	P.R.	DEBIT	CREDIT	BALANCE

DATE	EXPLANATION	P.R.	DEBIT	CREDIT	BALANCE

ACCOUNTS PAYABLE LEDGER

DATE	EXPLANATION	P.R.	DEBIT	CREDIT	BALANCE

DATE	EXPLANATION	P.R.	DEBIT	CREDIT	BALANCE

DATE	EXPLANATION	P.R.	DEBIT	CREDIT	BALANCE

DATE	EXPLANATION	P.R.	DEBIT	CREDIT	BALANCE

Company	Accounting System Computerized	Software Used	Input Device(s)	On-line or Batch	Network or Workstations

(1) _____
_____
_____
_____
_____
_____
_____

(2) _____
_____
_____
_____
_____
_____
_____

(3) _____
_____
_____
_____
_____
_____
_____

_____
_____
_____
_____
_____
_____
_____
_____
_____
_____

Quick Study 9-2

(a) _____
_____
_____
_____
_____
_____
_____

(b) _____
_____
_____
_____
_____
_____
_____

Quick Study 9-3

(1) _____
_____

(2) _____
_____

(3) _____
_____

(a) (1) Establishment of the Fund:

GENERAL JOURNAL

Date	Account Titles and Explanation	Post Ref.	Debit	Credit

(2) Reimbursement of the Fund at Month-End:

GENERAL JOURNAL

Date	Account Titles and Explanation	Post Ref.	Debit	Credit

(b) _____
_____
_____
_____

Quick Study 9-5
Parts a. and b.

	Bank or Book Effect	Add or Subtract	Journal Entry Required or Not
(1)			
(2)			
(3)			
(4)			
(5)			
(6)			
(7)			

_____
_____
_____
_____
_____
_____
_____
_____

Quick Study 9-7

Days' Sales Uncollected (2000): _____
_____
_____
_____
_____

Days' Sales Uncollected (1999): _____
_____
_____
_____
_____

Interpretation and Explanation: _____
_____
_____
_____
_____

Exercise 9-1

_____
_____
_____
_____
_____
_____
_____
_____
_____
_____
_____

(a) _____
_____
_____
_____
_____
_____
_____

(b) _____
_____
_____
_____
_____
_____
_____

Exercise 9-3

Internal Control Problem: _____
_____
_____
_____
_____
_____
_____
_____
_____

Internal Control Recommendation: _____
_____
_____
_____
_____
_____
_____

Exercise 9-4
(a) Establish the Fund

GENERAL JOURNAL

Date	Account Titles and Explanation	Post Ref.	Debit	Credit

(b) Reimburse the Fund

GENERAL JOURNAL

Date	Account Titles and Explanation	Post Ref.	Debit	Credit

(c) Reimburse and Increase the Fund

GENERAL JOURNAL

Date	Account Titles and Explanation	Post Ref.	Debit	Credit

Exercise 9-5

(a) Establish the Fund

GENERAL JOURNAL

Date	Account Titles and Explanation	Post Ref.	Debit	Credit

(b) Reimburse and Reduce the Fund

GENERAL JOURNAL

Date	Account Titles and Explanation	Post Ref.	Debit	Credit

Exercise 9-6

Exercise 9-7

GENERAL JOURNAL

Date	Account Titles and Explanation	Post Ref.	Debit	Credit

	Bank Balance		Book Balance			Not Shown on the Reconciliation
	Add	Deduct	Add	Deduct	Adjust	
1. Interest earned on the account.						
2. Deposit made on September 30 after the bank was closed.						
3. Checks outstanding on August 31 that cleared the bank in September.						
4. NSF check from customer returned on September 15 but not recorded by the company						
5. Checks written and mailed to payees on September 30.						
6. Deposit made on September 5 that was processed on September 8.						
7. Bank service charge.						
8. Checks written and mailed to payees on October 5.						
9. Check written by another depositor but charged against the company's account.						
10. Principal and interest collected by the bank but not recorded by the company.						
11. Special charge for collection of note in No. 10 on company's behalf.						
12. Check written against the account and cleared by the bank; erroneously omitted by the company recordkeeper.						

(a) Recording Invoices at Gross Amounts

GENERAL JOURNAL

Date	Account Titles and Explanation	Post Ref.	Debit	Credit

(b) Recording Invoices at Net Amounts

GENERAL JOURNAL

Date	Account Titles and Explanation	Post Ref.	Debit	Credit

Days' Sales Uncollected (1999): _____
_____
_____
_____

Days' Sales Uncollected (2000): _____
_____
_____
_____

Interpretation of Changes in Liquidity: _____
_____
_____
_____
_____

GENERAL JOURNAL

Date	Account Titles and Explanation	Post Ref.	Debit	Credit

Part 2

Part 3

GENERAL JOURNAL

Date	Account Titles and Explanation	Post Ref.	Debit	Credit

GENERAL JOURNAL

Date	Account Titles and Explanation	Post Ref.	Debit	Credit

Part 2

Part 2

GENERAL JOURNAL

Date	Account Titles and Explanation	Post Ref.	Debit	Credit

_____
_____
_____
_____
_____
_____
_____
_____
_____
_____
_____
_____
_____

Problem 9-4 or 9-4A
Part 1

_____
_____

GENERAL JOURNAL

Date	Account Titles and Explanation	Post Ref.	Debit	Credit

Part 3

(1) _____

_____

(2) _____

_____

(3) _____

_____

Problem 9-5 or 9-5A

(1) Principle Violated:
Recommendation:

(2) **Principle Violated:**
Recommendation:

(3) **Principle Violated:**
Recommendation:

(4) **Principle Violated:**
Recommendation:

(5) **Principle Violated:**
Recommendation:

Reporting in Action

Part 1

Item	May 31, 1997 Balance ($)	Cash & Equiv. as % of Balance	May 31, 1996 Balance ($)	Cash & Equiv. as % of Balance

Interpretation: _____

_____

_____
_____
_____
_____
_____
_____
_____
_____

Part 3
Days' Sales Uncollected (May 31, 1997): _____
_____
_____
_____

Days' Sales Uncollected (May 31, 1996): _____
_____
_____
_____

Interpretation: _____
_____
_____
_____
_____

Part 4
Days' Sales Uncollected (**):** _____
_____
_____
_____

Interpretation: _____
_____
_____
_____
_____

Nike:
Days' Sales Uncollected (May 31, 1997): _____
_____
_____

Days' Sales Uncollected (May 31, 1996): _____
_____
_____

Interpretation: _____
_____
_____
_____

Reebok:
Days' Sales Uncollected (December 31, 1996): _____
_____
_____

Days' Sales Uncollected (December 31, 1995): _____
_____
_____

Interpretation: _____
_____
_____
_____

Comparison – NIKE vs. Reebok: _____
_____
_____

(1) _____

_____

_____

_____

_____

(2) _____

_____

_____

_____

_____

(3) _____

_____

_____

_____

_____

_____

_____

_____

(4) _____

_____

_____

_____

_____

_____

_____

_____

MEMORANDUM

TO:

FROM:

SUBJECT:

DATE:

(1) _____
_____
_____
_____
_____
_____

(2) _____
_____
_____
_____
_____

(3) _____
_____
_____
_____
_____

(4) _____
_____
_____
_____
_____

(5) _____
_____
_____
_____
_____

Internal Controls Identified:

(1) _____

(2) _____

(3) _____

(4) _____

(5) _____

(6) _____

(7) _____

(8) _____

(9) _____

(10) _____

***Business Week* Activity**

(1) _____
_____
_____

(2) _____
_____
_____

(3) _____
_____
_____

GENERAL JOURNAL

Date	Account Titles and Explanation	Post Ref.	Debit	Credit

Quick Study 10-2
(a)

GENERAL JOURNAL

Date	Account Titles and Explanation	Post Ref.	Debit	Credit

(b)

GENERAL JOURNAL

Date	Account Titles and Explanation	Post Ref.	Debit	Credit

(a)

GENERAL JOURNAL

Date	Account Titles and Explanation	Post Ref.	Debit	Credit

(b)

GENERAL JOURNAL

Date	Account Titles and Explanation	Post Ref.	Debit	Credit

Quick Study 10-4

(a)

GENERAL JOURNAL

Date	Account Titles and Explanation	Post Ref.	Debit	Credit

(b) _____

_____

(c) _____

_____

_____

GENERAL JOURNAL

Date	Account Titles and Explanation	Post Ref.	Debit	Credit

Quick Study 10-6

GENERAL JOURNAL

Date	Account Titles and Explanation	Post Ref.	Debit	Credit

Quick Study 10-7

Accounts Receivable Turnover:

GENERAL JOURNAL

Date	Account Titles and Explanation	Post Ref.	Debit	Credit

GENERAL JOURNAL

Date	Account Titles and Explanation	Post Ref.	Debit	Credit

GENERAL LEDGER

Accounts Receivable	Sales	Sales Returns and Allowances

ACCOUNTS RECEIVABLE LEDGER

ABC Shop	Colt Enterprises	Red McKenzie

Part 2

Comparison:

GENERAL JOURNAL

Date	Account Titles and Explanation	Post Ref.	Debit	Credit

(a)

GENERAL JOURNAL

Date	Account Titles and Explanation	Post Ref.	Debit		Credit	

(b)

GENERAL JOURNAL

Date	Account Titles and Explanation	Post Ref.	Debit		Credit	

Exercise 10-6

GENERAL JOURNAL

Date	Account Titles and Explanation	Post Ref.	Debit		Credit	

GENERAL JOURNAL

Date	Account Titles and Explanation	Post Ref.	Debit	Credit

Exercise 10-8

GENERAL JOURNAL

Date	Account Titles and Explanation	Post Ref.	Debit	Credit

Financial Statement Note(s): _____

_____

_____

_____

Accounts Receivable Turnover (2000): _____
_____
_____
_____

Accounts Receivable Turnover (2001): _____
_____
_____
_____

Comparison and Interpretation: _____
_____
_____
_____

GENERAL JOURNAL

Date	Account Titles and Explanation	Post Ref.	Debit	Credit

GENERAL JOURNAL

Date	Account Titles and Explanation	Post Ref.	Debit	Credit

GENERAL JOURNAL

Date	Account Titles and Explanation	Post Ref.	Debit	Credit

GENERAL JOURNAL

Date	Account Titles and Explanation	Post Ref.	Debit	Credit
(a)				
(b)				
(c)				

Part 2

	Debit	Credit

Problem 10-4 or 10-4A
Part 1

Part 2

GENERAL JOURNAL

Date	Account Titles and Explanation	Post Ref.	Debit	Credit

Part 3

1999

GENERAL JOURNAL

Date	Account Titles and Explanation	Post Ref.	Debit	Credit

2000

GENERAL JOURNAL

Date	Account Titles and Explanation	Post Ref.	Debit	Credit

Date	Account Titles and Explanation	Post Ref.	Debit	Credit

Date	Account Titles and Explanation	Post Ref.	Debit			Credit		

Part 2

Reporting: _____

_____

_____

Reasoning: _____

_____

_____

_____

Principle: _____

_____

_____

_____

GENERAL JOURNAL

Date	Account Titles and Explanation	Post Ref.	Debit	Credit

Date	Account Titles and Explanation	Post Ref.	Debit	Credit

(1) _____

_____

(2) Liquid Assets Percent of Current Liabilities (May 31, 1997):

_____

_____

_____

Liquid Assets Percent of Current Liabilities (May 31, 1996):

_____

_____

_____

Comparison and Interpretation:

_____

_____

_____

_____

(3) _____

_____

_____

_____

(4) Accounts Receivable Turnover (May 31, 1997):

_____

_____

(5) Swoosh Ahead:

_____

_____

_____

_____

_____

_____

_____

_____

_____

_____

_____

_____

(1) NIKE's Accounts Receivable Turnover (May 31, 1997):

_____

_____

_____

_____

Reebok's Accounts Receivable Turnover (December 31, 1996):

_____

_____

_____

_____

_____

(2) NIKE:

_____

_____

Reebok:

_____

_____

(3) Efficiency Comparison:

_____

_____

(4) NIKE:

_____

_____

_____

Reebok:

_____

_____

Comparison:

_____

_____

_____

Name _____

(1) _____
_____
_____
_____
_____
_____
_____
_____

(2) _____
_____
_____
_____
_____
_____
_____
_____
_____

(3) _____
_____
_____
_____
_____
_____
_____
_____

MEMORANDUM

TO:

FROM:

SUBJECT:

DATE:

(1) _____
_____
_____
_____
_____
_____
_____
_____
_____

(2) _____
_____
_____
_____
_____
_____
_____
_____
_____

(3) _____
_____
_____
_____
_____
_____
_____
_____
_____

Estimate of Uncollectibles: _____

_____

_____

_____

_____

_____

_____

_____

Adjusting Entry:

GENERAL JOURNAL

Date	Account Titles and Explanation	Post Ref.	Debit	Credit

Presentation of Net Realizable Accounts Receivable:

Hitting the Road

Company	Credit Cards Accepted	Reasons

(1) _____
_____
_____

(2) _____
_____
_____
_____
_____

(3) _____
_____
_____
_____
_____

(4) _____
_____
_____
_____
_____

(5) _____
_____
_____
_____
_____

(a) _____
_____
_____
_____

(b) _____
_____
_____
_____

(c) _____
_____
_____
_____

Quick Study 11-2

_____
_____
_____
_____
_____
_____
_____
_____

Quick Study 11-3

(a) Straight-line: _____
_____

(b) Units-of-Production: _____
_____
_____
_____

Quick Study 11-4

Revised Straight-Line: _____
_____
_____
_____
_____

First Year: _____

_____

Second Year: _____

_____

Third Year: _____

_____

Quick Study 11-6

(a)
(1) _____
(2) _____
(3) _____
(4) _____

(b)

GENERAL JOURNAL

Date	Account Titles and Explanation	Post Ref.	Debit	Credit

Quick Study 11-7

GENERAL JOURNAL

Date	Account Titles and Explanation	Post Ref.	Debit	Credit

GENERAL JOURNAL

Date	Account Titles and Explanation	Post Ref.	Debit	Credit
(a)				
(b)				

Quick Study 11-9

(1) _____

(2) _____

(3) _____

(4) _____

Quick Study 11-10

_____

_____

_____

_____

_____

_____

GENERAL JOURNAL

Date	Account Titles and Explanation	Post Ref.	Debit	Credit
(a)				
(b)				

Quick Study 11-12

Intangible Asset(s): _____

Natural Resource(s): _____

Quick Study 11-13

GENERAL JOURNAL

Date	Account Titles and Explanation	Post Ref.	Debit	Credit

_____
_____
_____
_____
_____
_____
_____
_____
_____
_____

Exercise 11-2

Allocation of Costs to Assets: _____
_____
_____
_____
_____
_____
_____
_____
_____
_____

GENERAL JOURNAL

Date	Account Titles and Explanation	Post Ref.	Debit			Credit		

Cost of Assets: _____

_____
_____
_____
_____
_____
_____
_____

GENERAL JOURNAL

Date	Account Titles and Explanation	Post Ref.	Debit	Credit

Exercise 11-4

Straight-Line: _____

_____
_____
_____

Units-of-Production: _____

_____
_____
_____

Double-Declining Balance: _____

_____
_____
_____
_____

Straight-Line:

_____
_____
_____

Double-Declining-Balance:

_____
_____
_____
_____
_____
_____

Exercise 11-6

(a) _____
_____
_____
_____
_____

(b) _____
_____
_____
_____
_____
_____

(a) Straight-Line Depreciation:

Year	Income before Depreciation	Depreciation Expense	Net Income

(b) Double-Declining-Balance Depreciation:

Year	Income before Depreciation	Depreciation Expense	Net Income

(a) Straight-Line Depreciation:

Year	Annual Depreciation	Ending Book Value

(b) Double-Declining-Balance Depreciation:

Year	Beginning Book Value	Annual Percent	Annual Depreciation	Ending Book Value

Exercise 11-9

GENERAL JOURNAL

Date	Account Titles and Explanation	Post Ref.	Debit	Credit
(a)				
(b)				
(c)				

(a) _____

_____

_____

_____

_____

(b)

GENERAL JOURNAL

Date	Account Titles and Explanation	Post Ref.	Debit	Credit

(c) _____

_____

_____

_____

_____

_____

(d)

GENERAL JOURNAL

Date	Account Titles and Explanation	Post Ref.	Debit	Credit

GENERAL JOURNAL

Date	Account Titles and Explanation	Post Ref.	Debit			Credit		
(a)								
(b)								

Computations:

Exercise 11-12

(a) _____

_____

_____

(b) _____

_____

_____

(c) _____

_____

_____

_____

GENERAL JOURNAL

Date	Account Titles and Explanation	Post Ref.	Debit	Credit
(a)				
(b)				
(c)				
(d)				

Exercise 11-14

(a) _____

(b) _____

(c) _____

(d) _____

(e) _____

Total Asset Turnover (1999):

Total Asset Turnover (2000):

Efficiency Analysis:

Exercise 11-16

GENERAL JOURNAL

Date	Account Titles and Explanation	Post Ref.	Debit	Credit

Exercise 11-17

GENERAL JOURNAL

Date	Account Titles and Explanation	Post Ref.	Debit	Credit

(a) Value of Goodwill: _____
_____
_____
_____
_____
_____

(b) Value of Goodwill: _____
_____
_____
_____
_____
_____

Problem 11-1 or 11-1A

Part 1

	Land	Building Two (or B)	Building Three (or C)	Land Improv. One (or B)	Land Improv. Two (or C)
Purchase price					
Demolition............ ...					
Landscaping					
New building............					
New improvements .	_____	_____	_____	_____	_____
Totals	_____	_____	_____	_____	_____

Computations:

GENERAL JOURNAL

Date	Account Titles and Explanation	Post Ref.	Debit	Credit

Part 3

GENERAL JOURNAL

Date	Account Titles and Explanation	Post Ref.	Debit	Credit

	Appraised Value	Percent of Total	Apportioned Cost
Building			
Land			
Land improvements			
Vehicles			
Total			

GENERAL JOURNAL

Date	Account Titles and Explanation	Post Ref.	Debit	Credit

Part 2

_____
_____
_____
_____

Part 3

_____
_____
_____
_____
_____

Part 4

_____
_____
_____
_____
_____
_____
_____

Year	Straight-Line(a)	Units-of-Production(b)	Double-Declining-Balance(c)
1			
2			
3			
4			
5 (for 11-3A)	_____	_____	_____
Totals	_____	_____	_____

Workspace:
(a) Straight-Line: _____
_____
_____

(b) Units-of-Production: _____
_____
_____
_____
_____
_____

(c) Double-Declining-Balance: _____
_____
_____
_____
_____
_____

Part 2
(a)

GENERAL JOURNAL

Date	Account Titles and Explanation	Post Ref.	Debit	Credit

(b)

GENERAL JOURNAL

Date	Account Titles and Explanation	Post Ref.	Debit		Credit	

(c)

GENERAL JOURNAL

Date	Account Titles and Explanation	Post Ref.	Debit		Credit	
(i) Sold for $_____ cash:						
(ii) Sold for $_____ cash:						
(iii) Destroyed in fire, collected $_____ cash from insurance						

Year 1999:

GENERAL JOURNAL

Date	Account Titles and Explanation	Post Ref.	Debit			Credit		

GENERAL JOURNAL

Date	Account Titles and Explanation	Post Ref.	Debit	Credit

Year 1999:

GENERAL JOURNAL

Date		Account Titles and Explanation	Post Ref.	Debit			Credit		

Year 2000:

GENERAL JOURNAL

Date		Account Titles and Explanation	Post Ref.	Debit			Credit		

GENERAL JOURNAL

Date	Account Titles and Explanation	Post Ref.	Debit	Credit

GENERAL JOURNAL

Date	Account Titles and Explanation	Post Ref.	Debit	Credit

Date	Account Titles and Explanation	Post Ref.	Debit	Credit

Problem 11-7 or 11-7A
Part 1

GENERAL JOURNAL

Date	Account Titles and Explanation	Post Ref.	Debit	Credit

Preparation Component

GENERAL JOURNAL

Date	Account Titles and Explanation	Post Ref.	Debit			Credit		

Analysis Component:

_____
_____
_____
_____
_____
_____
_____
_____

Problem 11-8 or 11-8A
Part 1

_____
_____
_____
_____
_____
_____
_____
_____
_____

_____
_____
_____
_____
_____
_____
_____
_____

Part 3

_____
_____
_____
_____
_____
_____
_____
_____

Part 4

_____
_____
_____
_____
_____
_____
_____

Reporting in Action

(1) _____
_____
_____
_____
_____
_____
_____
_____

(2) _____
_____
_____
_____
_____

(3) _____
_____
_____
_____
_____

(4) _____
_____
_____
_____
_____

(5) Swoosh Ahead: _____
_____
_____
_____
_____

Comparative Analysis

(1) Total Asset Turnover (NIKE): _____
_____
_____

Total Asset Turnover (Reebok): _____
_____
_____

(2) Efficiency Analysis: _____
_____
_____
_____

(1) _____
_____
_____
_____
_____
_____
_____
_____
_____
_____
_____

(2) _____
_____
_____
_____
_____
_____
_____
_____
_____
_____

(3) _____
_____
_____
_____
_____
_____
_____
_____
_____
_____

Total Asset Turnover	Company 1	Company 2	Company 3	Company 4	Company 5	Average
DATA FOR MEMORANDUM						

MEMORANDUM

TO:

FROM:

SUBJECT:

DATE:

Patents:	Product (1) _____	Product (2) _____	Product (3) _____
1. _____			
2. _____			
3. _____			
4. _____			
5. _____			
6. _____			
7. _____			
8. _____			
9. _____			
10. _____			

Presentation Outline

Method of Expertise: _____
_____
_____
_____
_____

(a) Depreciation Expense: _____
_____
_____
_____
_____
_____
_____

(b) Explanations: _____
_____
_____
_____
_____
_____

(c) Analysis Versus Other Methods: _____
_____
_____
_____
_____
_____

(d) Book Value and Reporting: _____
_____
_____
_____
_____
_____

Asset	Company	Cost Allocation Method
Natural Resource		
Patent		
Lease		
Leasehold Improvement		
Copyright		
Trademark		
Goodwill		

Business Week Activity

(1) _____
_____
_____
_____
_____

(2) _____
_____
_____
_____
_____

(3) _____
_____
_____
_____

(4) _____
_____
_____
_____
_____

Current Liabilities:

Quick Study 12-2

GENERAL JOURNAL

Date	Account Titles and Explanation	Post Ref.	Debit	Credit

Quick Study 12-3

GENERAL JOURNAL

Date	Account Titles and Explanation	Post Ref.	Debit	Credit

Quick Study 12-4

(a) Accrued Interest Payable:

(b)

GENERAL JOURNAL

Date	Account Titles and Explanation	Post Ref.	Debit	Credit

Quick Study 12-5

GENERAL JOURNAL

Date	Account Titles and Explanation	Post Ref.	Debit	Credit

GENERAL JOURNAL

Date		Account Titles and Explanation	Post Ref.	Debit			Credit		

Quick Study 12-7

(1) _____

(2) _____

(3) _____

Quick Study 12-8

GENERAL JOURNAL

Date		Account Titles and Explanation	Post Ref.	Debit			Credit		

GENERAL JOURNAL

Date	Account Titles and Explanation	Post Ref.	Debit	Credit

Quick Study 12-10

Times Interest Earned: _____

_____

_____

_____

Exercise 12-1

(a) _____   (f) _____

(b) _____   (g) _____

(c) _____   (h) _____

(d) _____   (i) _____

(e) _____   (j) _____

Exercise 12-2

(a) _____

_____

(b) _____

_____

(c) _____

_____

(d) _____

_____

(e)

GENERAL JOURNAL

Date	Account Titles and Explanation	Post Ref.	Debit	Credit

Exercise 12-3

(1) _____

_____

_____

_____

_____

(2)

GENERAL JOURNAL

Date	Account Titles and Explanation	Post Ref.	Debit	Credit

	Subject to Tax	Rate	Tax

(a)

FICA--Social Security .... _____ _____ _____

FICA--Medicare .... _____ _____ _____

FUTA .... _____ _____ _____

SUTA .... _____ _____ _____

(b)

FICA--Social Security .... _____ _____ _____

FICA--Medicare .... _____ _____ _____

FUTA .... _____ _____ _____

SUTA .... _____ _____ _____

(c)

FICA--Social Security .... _____ _____ _____

FICA--Medicare .... _____ _____ _____

FUTA .... _____ _____ _____

SUTA _____ _____ _____

Exercise 12-5

GENERAL JOURNAL

Date	Account Titles and Explanation	Post Ref.	Debit	Credit

Name _____

(a) Maturity Date: _____

(b) Interest Expense: _____

_____

_____

_____

(c)

GENERAL JOURNAL

Date	Account Titles and Explanation	Post Ref.	Debit	Credit

(d)

GENERAL JOURNAL

Date	Account Titles and Explanation	Post Ref.	Debit	Credit

(a) Maturity Date: _____
_____
_____
_____

(b) Interest Expense (1999): _____
_____
_____
_____
_____

(c) Interest Expense (2000): _____
_____
_____
_____
_____

(d)

GENERAL JOURNAL

Date	Account Titles and Explanation	Post Ref.	Debit	Credit

(e)

GENERAL JOURNAL

Date	Account Titles and Explanation	Post Ref.	Debit	Credit

GENERAL JOURNAL

Date	Account Titles and Explanation	Post Ref.	Debit	Credit
(1)				
(2)				
(3)				
(4)				
(5)				
(6)				

_____
_____
_____

Exercise 12-10

(a) _____
_____

(b) _____
_____

(c) _____
_____

(d) _____
_____

(e) _____
_____

(f) _____
_____

Analysis: _____
_____
_____

Name _____

Exercise 12-11

_____
_____
_____
_____
_____
_____
_____
_____
_____
_____
_____
_____

GENERAL JOURNAL

Date	Account Titles and Explanation	Post Ref.	Debit			Credit		

Exercise 12-13

_____
_____
_____
_____
_____
_____
_____
_____
_____
_____
_____

(1) Warranty Expense for November and December 1999:

_____
_____
_____
_____
_____
_____

(2) Warranty Expense for January 2000:

_____
_____
_____
_____
_____
_____
_____

(3) Balance of the Estimated Warranty Liability as of December 31, 1999:

_____
_____
_____
_____
_____
_____

(4) Balance of the Estimated Warranty Liability as of January 31, 2000:

_____
_____
_____
_____
_____
_____
_____

(5)

GENERAL JOURNAL

Date	Account Titles and Explanation	Post Ref.	Debit	Credit

(1) Maturity Dates:

_____
_____
_____
_____
_____
_____

(2) Interest Due at Maturity:

_____
_____
_____
_____
_____
_____
_____

(3) Accrued Interest at the End of 1999:

_____
_____
_____
_____
_____
_____

(4) Interest Expense in 2000:

_____
_____
_____
_____
_____
_____

(5)

GENERAL JOURNAL

Date	Account Titles and Explanation	Post Ref.	Debit	Credit

(1) Each Employee's FICA Withholdings for Social Security:

_____   _____   _____   _____   **Total**

_____
_____
_____
_____
_____
_____
_____
_____
_____
_____

(2) Each Employee's FICA Withholdings for Medicare:

_____   _____   _____   _____   **Total**

_____
_____
_____
_____
_____

(3) Employer's FICA Taxes for Social Security:

_____   _____   _____   _____   **Total**

_____
_____
_____

(4) Employer's FICA Taxes for Medicare:

_____   _____   _____   _____   **Total**

_____
_____
_____
_____

(5) Employer's FUTA Taxes:

_____ _____ _____ _____   Total

_____
_____
_____
_____
_____
_____
_____
_____
_____

(6) Employer's SUTA Taxes:

_____ _____ _____ _____   Total

_____
_____
_____
_____

(7) Each Employee's Take-Home Pay:

_____ _____ _____ _____   Total

_____
_____
_____
_____
_____
_____
_____
_____

(8) Employer's Total Payroll-Related Expense for Each Employee:

_____ _____ _____ _____   Total

_____
_____
_____
_____
_____
_____
_____
_____
_____

(1) _____ **Company:**

Times Interest Earned: _____

_____

_____

_____

_____

(2) _____ **Company:**

Times Interest Earned: _____

_____

_____

_____

_____

(3) Sales Increase by _____%:

_____   _____

_____

_____

_____

_____

_____

_____

_____

_____

(4) Sales Increase by _____%:

_____   _____

_____

_____

_____

_____

_____

_____

_____

(5) Sales Increase by _____%:

_____   _____

(6) Sales Decrease by _____%:

_____   _____

(7) Sales Decrease by _____%:

_____   _____

(8) Sales Decrease by _____%:

_____   _____

(9) Analysis:

GENERAL JOURNAL

Date	Account Titles and Explanation	Post Ref.	Debit	Credit

(1)

GENERAL JOURNAL

Date	Account Titles and Explanation	Post Ref.	Debit	Credit

(2)

GENERAL JOURNAL

Date	Account Titles and Explanation	Post Ref.	Debit	Credit

(3)

GENERAL JOURNAL

Date	Account Titles and Explanation	Post Ref.	Debit	Credit

(4)

Comprehensive Problem
Part 1

(a) Correct Ending Balance of Cash and the Amount of the Omitted Check:

(b) Allowance for Doubtful Accounts:

(c) Depreciation Expense on the Truck:

(d) Depreciation Expense on the Equipment:

(e) Correct Revenue and Unearned Revenue Balances:

(f) Warranty Expense and Warranty Liability:

(g) Discount on Note Payable and Interest Expense:

AARDVARK EXTERMINATORS
Six-Column Table
December 31, 2000

Account Titles	Unadjusted Trial Balance Dr.	Unadjusted Trial Balance Cr.	Adjustments Dr.	Adjustments Cr.	Adjusted Trial Balance Dr.	Adjusted Trial Balance Cr.
Cash						
Accounts Receivable						
Allowance for Doubtful Accounts						
Merchandise Inventory						
Trucks						
Accumulated Depreciation, Trucks						
Equipment						
Accum. Depreciation, Equipment						
Accounts Payable						
Estimated Warranty Liability						
Unearned Services Revenue						
Long-Term Notes Payable						
Discount on Notes Payable						
K. Jones, Capital						
K. Jones, Withdrawals						
Extermination Services Revenue						
Interest Earned						
Sales						
Cost of Goods Sold						
Depreciation Expense, Trucks						
Depreciation Expense, Equipment						
Wages Expense						
Interest Expense						
Rent Expense						
Bad Debts Expense						
Miscellaneous Expense						
Repairs Expense						
Utilities Expense						
Warranty Expense						
Totals						

GENERAL JOURNAL

Date	Account Titles and Explanation	Post Ref.	Debit	Credit

AARDVARK EXTERMINATORS
Income Statement
For Year Ended December 31, 2000

AARDVARK EXTERMINATORS
Statement of Changes in Owner's Equity
For Year Ended December 31, 2000

AARDVARK EXTERMINATORS
Balance Sheet
December 31, 2000

Reporting in Action

(1) Times Interest Earned (May 31, 1997): _____

_____

_____

_____

_____

Times Interest Earned (May 31, 1996): _____

_____

_____

_____

_____

_____

Interpretation: _____

_____

_____

_____

_____

_____

(2) _____
_____
_____
_____

(3) _____
_____
_____
_____
_____
_____

(4) Swoosh Ahead:
_____
_____
_____
_____
_____
_____

Comparative Analysis

(1) NIKE's Times Interest Earned (May 31, 1997): _____
_____
_____

NIKE's Times Interest Earned (May 31, 1996): _____
_____
_____

Reebok's Times Interest Earned (December 31, 1996): _____
_____
_____

Reebok's Times Interest Earned (December 31, 1995): _____
_____
_____
_____

(2) Interpretation: _____

_____

_____

_____

_____

_____

Ethics Challenge

(1) _____

_____

_____

_____

_____

_____

_____

_____

_____

(2) _____

_____

_____

_____

_____

_____

_____

_____

_____

_____

_____

MEMORANDUM

TO:

FROM:

SUBJECT:

DATE:

_____
_____
_____
_____
_____
_____
_____
_____
_____
_____
_____
_____
_____
_____
_____
_____
_____
_____
_____
_____
_____
_____
_____
_____

Teamwork in Action

(1) _____
_____
_____
_____
_____
_____
_____
_____
_____
_____

(2)

GENERAL JOURNAL

Date	Account Titles and Explanation	Post Ref.	Debit	Credit

(3) Team Discussion.

(4)

GENERAL JOURNAL

Date	Account Titles and Explanation	Post Ref.	Debit	Credit

(5) Team Discussion.

Complete the Personal Earnings and Benefits Estimate Form.

Business Week Activity

(1) _____
_____
_____
_____
_____
_____
_____

(2) _____
_____
_____
_____
_____
_____
_____

(3) _____
_____
_____
_____
_____
_____

(4) _____
_____
_____
_____
_____
_____
_____

(1) _____
(2) _____
(3) _____
(4) _____
(5) _____
(6) _____
(7) _____

Quick Study B-2

(1) _____
(2) _____
(3) _____
(4) _____
(5) _____
(6) _____
(7) _____
(8) _____
(9) _____

Quick Study B-3

Account Balances Most Likely to Mislead Users When Prices Change:
_____
_____
_____
_____
_____

Exercise B-1

(1) _____
(2) _____
(3) _____
(4) _____
(5) _____
(6) _____

Report on Prescriptive and Descriptive Concepts

Name _____

Account Balances That Are Likely to Markedly Change if a Mark to Market Basis Were Applied to NIKE's Balance Sheet:

_____
_____
_____
_____
_____
_____
_____

Exercise B-4

Accounts	Sources of Market Value Information
Inventory..	_____
	_____
	_____
	_____
Land	_____
	_____
	_____
	_____
	_____
Equipment	_____
	_____
	_____
	_____
	_____
Short-Term Stock Investments	_____
	_____
	_____
	_____
	_____

(a) _____
(b) _____
(c) _____
(d) _____

Quick Study C-2

Value of Investment: _____
_____
_____
_____

Quick Study C-3

Cash Proceeds: _____
_____
_____
_____

Quick Study C-4

Value of Investment: _____
_____
_____
_____

Quick Study C-5

Future Value of Retirement Program: _____
_____
_____
_____

Quick Study C-6

Annual Rate of Interest Earned: _____
_____
_____
_____

Years of Investment: _____

_____

_____

_____

Exercise C-1

	Present or Future Value	Single Amount or Annuity	Relevant Table	Interest Rate	Number of Periods
(a)					
(b)					
(c)					
(d)					

Exercise C-2

Years Until Payment: _____

_____

_____

Exercise C-3

Rate of Interest Earned: _____

_____

_____

Exercise C-4

Rate of Interest Earned: _____

_____

_____

Appendix C   **Exercise C-5**   *Name* _____

Number of Annual Payments Received: _____
_____
_____
_____

Exercise C-6

Rate of Interest Earned: _____
_____
_____
_____

Exercise C-7

Number of Annual Investments: _____
_____
_____
_____

Exercise C-8

Cost of Automobile: _____
_____
_____
_____
_____
_____

Exercise C-9

Total Amount in the Account: _____
_____
_____
_____
_____
_____

Name _____

Total Accumulated in the Account: _____
_____
_____
_____
_____
_____
_____

Exercise C-11

Cash Proceeds from Bond: _____
_____
_____
_____
_____
_____
_____
_____
_____

Exercise C-12

Future Value of the Fund: _____
_____
_____
_____
_____
_____
_____
_____

Exercise C-13

Present Value of Investment: _____
_____
_____
_____

Exercise C-14

Future Value of Investment: _____
_____
_____
_____

Fundamental Accounting Principles, 15th Edition

(a)

(b)

Exercise C-16

Amount Borrowed:

Exercise C-17

(a)

(b)

(c)

(d)

(e)

(f)

(a) First Annuity:

_____
_____
_____
_____
_____
_____
_____

Second Annuity:

_____
_____
_____
_____
_____
_____

(b) First Annuity:

_____
_____
_____

Second Annuity:

_____
_____
_____
_____

Exercise C-19

(a) _____
_____
_____
_____

(b) _____
_____
_____
_____

(c) _____
_____
_____
_____